Contents

WELCOME to our one year anniversary of the magazine formerly known as Treazine. We've got a new look, a new name and a new focus on print media. Introducing JOHNSTONE, an old-school print publication — no color, no links, no bullshit. Print it out and enjoy in the sunlight with coffee.*

Our distribution model is best described as consensual bootlegging. Everything within this magazine is copyright free, and you can do what you like with it — up to and including downloading the file, printing it, distributing it, and selling it for your own profit. Turn to page 58 for more details on how you can distribute JOHNSTONE yourself. If you still need help or reassurance, email us: admin@caitlinjohnstone.com

All works are written by Caitlin Johnstone and Tim Foley. The Caitlin Johnstone project is 100 percent reader-funded.

*serving suggestion only

Australia Agrees To Build US Missiles; US Dismisses Australian Concerns About Assange

Two different news stories about US-Australian relations have broken at around the same time, and together they sum up the story of US-Australian relations as a whole. In one we learn that Australia has agreed to manufacture missiles for the United States, and in the other we learn that Washington has told Australia to go suck eggs about its concerns regarding the US persecution of Australian journalist Julian Assange.

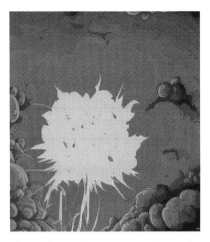

The relationship between Australia and the United States is all the more clearly illustrated by the way they are being reported by Australia's embarrassingly sycophantic mainstream press.

In a Sydney Morning Herald article published Friday titled "'Hugely significant': Australia to manufacture and export missiles to US," the US-educated war propagandist Matthew Knott exuberantly reports on the latest development on Australia's total absorption into the American war machine.

"Australia is set to begin manufacturing its own missiles within two years under an ambitious plan that will allow the country to supply guided weapons to the United States and possibly export them to other nations," Knott reports," adding that the "joint missile manufacturing effort is being driven by the war in Ukraine, which has highlighted a troubling lack of ammunition stocks in Western nations including the US."

Knott—perhaps best-known for being publicly told to "hang your head in shame" and "drum yourself out of Australian journalism" by former prime minister Paul Keating over his virulent war propaganda on China—gushes enthusiastically about the wonderful opportunities this southward expansion of the military-industrial complex will offer Australians.

"As well as creating local jobs, a domestic missile manufacturing industry will make Australia less reliant on imports and provide a trusted additional source of munitions for the US," Knott writes ecstatically in what has somehow been presented by The Sydney Morning Herald as a hard news story and not an opinion piece.

An article published the next day, also in The Sydney Morning Herald and also by Matthew Knott, is titled "Assange 'endangered lives': Top official urges Australia to understand US concerns".

It's not unusual to see this type of propagandistic headline designed to convey a specific message above Knott's reporting on this subject; in 2019 he authored a piece which was given the bogus title "'A monster not a journalist': Mueller report shows Assange lied about Russian hacking".

"The United States' top foreign policy official has urged Australians to understand American concerns about Julian Assange's publishing of leaked classified information, saying the WikiLeaks founder is alleged to have endangered lives and put US national security at risk," Knott writes. "In the sharpest and most detailed remarks from a Biden administration official about the matter, US Secretary of State Antony Blinken said Assange had been involved in one of the largest breaches of classified information in American history and had been charged with serious criminal conduct in the US."

Blinken's remarks came during a press conference for the Australia–US Ministerial Consultations (AUSMIN) forum on Saturday, in response to a question asked by Knott himself.

Here are Blinken's comments in full:

"Look, as a general matter policy, we don't really comment on extradition matters, extradition proceedings. And so, I really would refer you to our Department of Justice for any questions about the status of the criminal case, whether it's with regard to Mr Assange or the other person in question. And I really do understand and can certainly confirm what Penny said about the fact that this matter was raised with us as it has been in the past. And I understand the sensitivities, I understand the concerns and views of Australians. I think it's very important that our friends here understand our concerns about this matter. And what our Department of Justice has already said repeatedly, publicly, is this, Mr Assange was charged with very serious criminal conduct in the United States in connection with his alleged role in one of the largest compromises of classified information in the history of our country. The actions that he is alleged to have committed risked very serious harm to our national security, to the benefit of our adversaries and put named human sources at grave risk, grave risk of physical harm, grave risk of detention. So, I say that only because, just as we understand sensitivities here, it's important that our friends understand sensitivities in the United States."

The reason Blinken keeps repeating the word "risk" here is because the Pentagon already publicly acknowledged in 2013 that nobody was actually harmed by the 2010 Manning leaks that Assange is being charged with publishing, so all US officials can do is make the unfalsifiable assertion that they could have potentially been harmed had things happened completely differently in some hypothetical alternate timeline.

In reality, Assange is being persecuted by the United States for no other reason than the crime of good journalism. His reporting exposed US war crimes, and the US wishes to set a legal precedent that allows for anyone who reveals such criminality to be imprisoned in the United States—not just the whistleblowers who bring forth that information, but publishers who circulate it. This is why even mainstream press outlets and human rights organizations unequivocally oppose his extradition; because it would be a devastating blow to worldwide press freedoms on what is arguably the single most important issue that journalists can possibly report on.

So here is Australia signing up to become the Pentagon's weapons supplier to the south—on top of already functioning as a total US military/intelligence asset which is preparing to back Washington in a war with China, and on top of being so fully prostrated before the empire that we're not even allowed to know if American nuclear weapons are in our own country—being publicly hand-waved away by Washington's top diplomat for expressing concern about a historic legal case in which an

Australian citizen is being persecuted by the world's most powerful government for being a good journalist.

You could not ask for a clearer illustration of the so-called "alliance" between Australia and the United States. It's easy to see that this is not an equal partnership between two sovereign nations, but a relationship of total domination and subservience. I was only half-joking when I wrote the other day that our national symbol should be the star-spangled kangaroo.

Australia is not a real country. It's a US military base with marsupials.

Image via Adobe Stock

Funny How The UFO Narrative Coincides With The Race To Weaponize Space

If Wednesday's House Oversight subcommittee hearing on UFOs had happened ten years ago instead of today, it would have shaken the world. Imagine someone from 2013 hearing congressional testimonies about "routine" military pilot encounters with giant flying tic tacs, floating orbs, 300-foot red squares, and cubes in clear spheres zipping around in ways that surpass all known earthly technology by leaps and bounds, or about secret government possession of otherworldly aircraft they're trying to reverse engineer and the dead bodies of their non-human pilots, or about the possibility that these creatures are not merely extraterrestrial but extra-dimensional. Their jaws would have hit the floor.

Now in 2023 we've been getting incrementally drip-fed bits and pieces of these stories for six years, so the scene on Capitol Hill on Wednesday didn't have the impact it would've had in 2013. It's making headlines and getting attention, but not as much as Sinead O'Connor's death or people's thoughts on Barbie and Oppenheimer. The response from the general public could be described as a collective nervous laugh and a shrug.

People scroll past the footage from the hearing on social media, go "Whoa, that's weird," and move on with their lives. The information's going in, but just kind of on the periphery of mainstream consciousness. Maybe next year they'll show us something that would've been even more shocking to someone in 2013 than Wednesday's hearing would've been, and it will be met with the same nervous laugh and shrug by the people of 2024.

Of course in the circles I tend to interact with, the response is a bit different. People who are highly skeptical of the US war machine tend to also be highly skeptical of this UFO narrative we've been seeing since 2017.

"Distraction" is a word you hear a lot. "It's just a distraction from ____", where "____" is whatever hot story they personally happen to be fascinated by at the moment. I personally don't buy that explanation; the new UFO narrative wasn't just cooked up at the last minute to distract from current headlines, it's been unfolding for six years, and people aren't even paying that much attention to it. The empire doesn't tend to orchestrate spectacular events as a "distraction" anyway; the adjustment of public attention tends to take the much more mundane form of agenda setting in the media, where some stories receive more attention than others based on what's convenient for the oligarchs who own the press.

I also see people theorizing that this is all a ploy to ramp up the US military budget. There could totally be something to that, but again this narrative has been unfolding for six years and so far the military budget has just been swelling in the usual yearly increments as always.

Don't get me wrong, though — I'm as skeptical about this thing as anyone. For one thing the origins of the mainstream UFO narrative which began in 2017 were steeped in extensive distortion, dishonesty and journalistic malpractice, and were carried forward by shady intelligence operatives like Lue Elizondo. David Grusch, who made by far the most sensational claims at Wednesday's congressional hearing with his tales of dead aliens and reverse-engineered UFOs, is himself an insider of the US intelligence cartel.

But for me what really stinks about all this UFO stuff is the timing. Here we are in the early stages of a new cold war which features a race to militarize space, and we're hearing congressional testimony about mysterious vehicles posing a threat to US airspace which have the ability to go up and down between earth and space very quickly. That smells off.

I mean, does it really sound like a coincidence that we're seeing all these news stories about UFOs and aliens at the same time we're seeing news stories about a race between the US and China and Russia to dominate space militarily? A Foreign Policy article from last year blares the headline "China and Russia Are Catching Up to U.S. in Space Capabilities, Pentagon Warns" with the subheading "The militarization of space is picking up pace." These warnings are echoed in articles by Defense One and Time. An article on the United Nations website from last year carries the title "'We Have Not Passed the Point of No Return', Disarmament Committee Told, Weighing Chance Outer Space

Could Become Next Battlefield." A 2021 report from the war machine-funded Center for Strategic and International Studies titled "Defense Against the Dark Arts in Space: Protecting Space Systems from Counterspace Weapons" warns of the urgent need to build more space weapons to counter US enemies. A Global Times article from last year carries the title "Chinese experts urge avoidance of space weaponization amid commercial space capability deployment in Ukraine."

These stories about the space militarization race aren't getting the attention the much more entertaining UFO stories are getting, but it seems likely that those who are responsible for moving the war machinery around are paying a lot more attention to the former than the latter. The US Space Force took its first steps toward becoming a reality in 2017, the same year these mainstream UFO stories started coming out, with the explicit purpose of countering Russia and China.

And it just seems mighty suspicious to me how we're being slowly paced into this UFO narrative (or UAP narrative for those hip to the current jargon) right when there's a mad rush to get weapons into space. I can't actually think of any other point in history when the timing of something like this would have looked *more* suspicious.

So for me the most disturbing parts of the UFO hearing were the parts that could wind up facilitating the agenda to militarize space, like when this phenomenon was framed as a "national security" threat or when it was mentioned that they can transition from earth to space very rapidly.

When asked by congressman Glenn Grothman "do you believe UAPs pose a threat to our national security?", former Navy commander David Fravor answered with an unequivocal yes. A few minutes later Fravor described these vehicles as being able to "come down from space, hang out for three hours and go back up."

When asked by congressman Andy Ogles whether UFOs could be "collecting reconnaissance information" on the US military, all three witnesses — Grusch, Fravor, and former Navy pilot Ryan Graves — answered in the affirmative. Asked by Ogles if UFOs could be "probing our capabilities," all three again said yes. Asked if UFOs could be "testing for vulnerabilities" in US military capabilities, all three again said yes. Asked if UFOs pose an existential threat to the national security of the United States, all three said they potentially do. Asked if there was any indication that UFOs are interested in US nuclear technology, all three said yes.

Ogles concluded his questioning by saying, "There clearly is a threat to the national security of the United States of America. As members of Congress, we have a responsibility to maintain oversight and be aware of these activities so that, if appropriate, we take action."

When asked by congressman Eric Burlison if "there has been activity by alien or non-human technology, and/or beings, that has caused harm to humans," Grusch said he couldn't get into specifics in a public setting (a common theme throughout the hearing), but said that "what I personally witnessed, myself and my wife, was very disturbing."

Grusch would complicate this cryptic statement a few minutes later by saying that he's never seen a UFO. How this statement doesn't contradict his previous statement about having witnessed harmful behavior from non-human technology and/or beings was not made clear.

So you've got US policymakers being told that there are vehicles using technology not of this world routinely violating US airspace and posing an existential threat to US national security, and that these craft can go from earth to space and back at will, and that they need to help make sure their nation can address this threat.

What conclusions do you come to when presented with that kind of information? If you're a lawmaker in charge of facilitating the operation of a highly militaristic empire, you're probably not going to conclude that it's time to hold hands and sing Kumbaya. You're probably eventually going to start thinking in terms of military technology.

One of the most important unanswered questions in all this UFO hullabaloo is, why now? Why are we seeing all this movement on "disclosure" after generations of zero movement? If these things are in fact real and the government has in fact been keeping them secret, why would the adamant policy of dismissal and locked doors suddenly be reversed, allowing "whistleblowers" to come forward and give testimony before congress? If they had motive to keep it a secret this entire time, why would that motive no longer be there?

If you ask the online UFO community, many will essentially take credit for the whole thing, saying the most powerful war machine ever assembled has reversed its policy of total opacity because of "pressure" applied by disclosure activists. This doesn't pass the smell test; the most powerful empire in history isn't reversing course on a longstanding policy of blanket secrecy because of internet forums and FOIA requests.

So why now? Why the drastic and sudden shift from UFOs and aliens being laughable tinfoil hat nonsense to the subject of serious congressional inquiries and widespread mainstream media coverage?

Well, the timing of the race to militarize space might provide an answer to the "why now?" question. Is it a coincidence that this new UFO narrative began its rollout in 2017, around the same time as the rollout of the Space Force? Are we being manipulated at mass scale about aliens and UFOs to help grease the wheels for the movement of war machinery into space? How likely is it that by pure coincidence this extraplanetary narrative timed out the way it did just as the US empire makes a last-ditch grab at unipolar planetary domination?

I don't know. I do know that if I'm assigning degrees of probability, *"Extraterrestrial or extradimensional beings are here and take a special interest in us and sometimes crash their vehicles and our government recovered them but kept them a secret but suddenly decided not to be so secretive about them anymore"* ranks significantly lower than *"Our rulers are lying and manipulating to advance their own interests again."*

I am 100 percent wide open to the possibility of extraterrestrials and otherworldly vehicles zipping around our atmosphere. What I am not open to is the claim that the most depraved institutions on earth have suddenly opened their mind to telling us the truth about these things, either out of the goodness of their hearts or because they were "pressured" by UFO disclosure activists.

I don't know what the hell is going on with this UFO thing, but I do know the drivers of the US empire have an extensive history of manipulating and deceiving at mass scale to advance imperial agendas. And I do know that at this crucial juncture in history where the empire is clinging to planetary domination with the tips of its fingernails, there are a lot of imperial agendas afoot.

Image via Adobe Stock

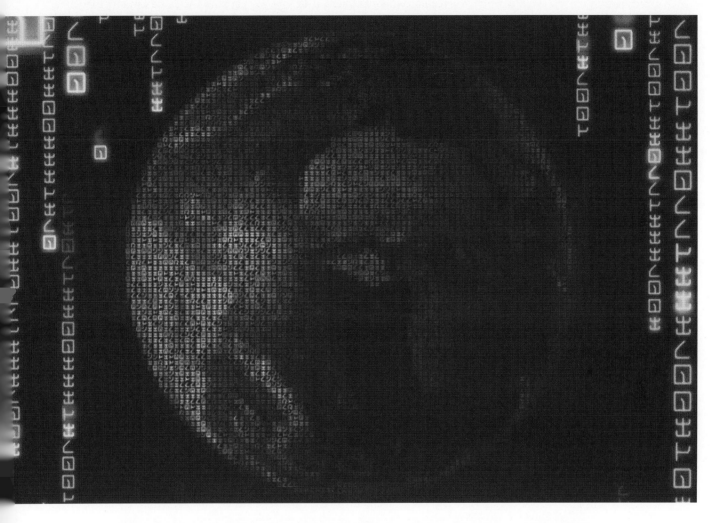

The Real World And The Narrative World

We each inhabit two very different worlds simultaneously: the real world, and the narrative world.

The real world is the physical world of matter, of atoms and molecules and stars and planets and animals wandering around trying to bite and copulate with each other. Science does not yet understand much of this world, but it can reasonably be said to have some degree of existence to it.

The narrative world is made of stories, of mental chatter about what's going on. It is only related to the real world in the loosest of terms, and commonly has no relation to the real world whatsoever.

In the narrative world you exist as a person with a certain name and a certain life story with a mountain of adjectives attached to you, some believed consciously and some believed subconsciously. You are this, you are that. You are inadequate. You are inferior. You are clever. You are fat. You are unlovable. Whatever. Words, words, words, words, words.

In the real world what you think of as "you" exists as an organism, breathing and digesting and pulsing and moving in the appearance of time. No thoughts or words need to occur for this organism to exist; it just is whatever it is.

In the narrative world, your surroundings are experienced as friends and foes, good and bad, right and wrong, threatening and non-threatening. Churning, babbling stories about what's happening pervade the experience of the narrative world: those people over there are bad people and should be punished. Those people over there are the good people and they should be rewarded. That man is blah blah blah. That woman is this and that.

In the real world, your surroundings are experienced as raw sensory data:

sensory impressions arising in each point in spacetime. Breath going in, breath going out. The feeling of feet on the ground. Sound of a bird call. Sight of a passing car. It's all just happening as it is, as whatever it is. Simple. Present.

In the narrative world, the United States changed dramatically on the 20th of January. If you live in one narrative echo chamber it changed dramatically for the better, if you live in the other narrative echo chamber it changed dramatically for the worse. But throughout the narrative world most agree that the 20th of January 2021 marked a very real and significant turn of events.

In the real world, things are moving in pretty much the same ways they were on January 19th. The money is moving in more or less the same directions at more or less the same rates. The weapons and troops are moving to more or less the same places in basically the same ways as before. The resources are behaving in essentially the same way. The people are moving in pretty much the same way. The actual, physical dynamics have remained predominantly unchanged.

The real world and the narrative world could not be more different. Skilled manipulators exploit these differences for their benefit like foreign exchange traders exploit the differences in world currency values. A religious manipulator can get you to hand over your real currency in exchange for narrative currency about eternal salvation or spiritual purification. A sexual predator can manipulate you into trading the real currency of sex for the narrative currency of "I think I'm in love with you". A politician can manipulate you into trading the real currency of votes

for the narrative currency of whatever they say on the campaign trail.

It's very hard to control people in the real world by just using the means that are available in the real world. If you're bigger and stronger than someone you can get them to hand over their sandwich by hitting them, or if you have a big stick or something. If you want to exert a large amount of control over a large number of people, though, you generally have to seize that control through the narrative world.

It's easier to control people through the narrative world than the real world because the narrative world and its relationship with the real world is too complicated for most people to understand, whereas the real world is quite simple and straightforward. For this reason, a tremendous amount of energy goes into controlling the dominant narratives, the dominant stories that people tell about what's going on in the world.

Convince people to accept the narrative that a government's leader is an evil dictator in need of regime change, and you can trade that narrative for real world control over a crucial geostrategic region. Convince people to accept that the status quo is working fine and any attempts to change it are dangerous insanity, and you ensure that people will never rise up and take away your real world control. Convince people that anyone questioning your narratives is a conspiracy theorist or a Russian propagandist, and you ensure your continued hegemonic control over the narrative world.

The most powerful manipulators are the ones who have succeeded in exerting control over both the real world and the narrative world, and they pursue both agendas with equal emphasis. Populations in the real world who insist upon their own national, resource, financial, economic or military sovereignty are subject to real world attacks by bombs, starvation sanctions and special ops. Entities in the narrative world which threaten imperial narrative domination are attacked, smeared, marginalized and censored.

That's all we are seeing with the increasingly shrill mainstream panic about disinformation, conspiracy theories, foreign propaganda and domestic extremism. Our rulers and their media lackeys are not compassionately protecting us from deception, they are ensuring that they remain the only ones authorized to administer deception. By golly the only ones allowed to deceive us should be our government, our news media, our teachers and our priests.

As China and its allies increasingly threaten the real world hegemony of the US and its allies, operations in the narrative world are getting increasingly heated and intense. Expect continued demonization of Russia, and expect anti-China propaganda to get more and more noisy. Expect people to be herded into partisan echo chambers with thicker and thicker walls in the narrative world, because dividing them up in this way makes it much easier to administer propaganda to them.

The narrative world is getting more and more frenzied while the real world is headed toward disaster due to the military and ecological pressures created by our status quo. There are only a few ways this can possibly break, with the most obvious being mass scale climate disaster or nuclear war.

There is also the possibility that the human species goes the other way and adapts. Organisms always wind up hitting a juncture where they either adapt to a new situation or go extinct, and we are approaching our juncture now.

Throughout recorded history, all around the globe, wise humans have been attesting that it is possible to transcend our delusion-rooted conditioning and come to a lucid perception of the narrative world and reality. There are many names for this lucid perception, but the one that caught on most widely is enlightenment.

We all have this potential within us. It has been gestating in us for many millennia. As we approach our adaptation-or-extinction juncture, we are very close indeed to learning if that potential will awaken in us or not.

If it does, a healthy and harmonious world will shift from being an unimaginable pipe dream to something very achievable. No longer confused about the relationship between the real world and the narrative world, we will be able to perceive our actual situation clearly, unfiltered by manipulation, and begin collaborating to build something beautiful and unprecedented. Once we move out of our narrative manipulation-driven model of competition and domination, and into a lucidity-driven model of collaboration with each other and with our ecosystem, a lasting peace will open up to us all.

.

Fifteen Useful Facts

1. It's easier to understand what's going on in the world when you mentally "mute" people's narratives about what's going on and just look at the material movements of wealth, resources, weapons, and people. That's how you separate what's real from the manipulations and empty narrative fluff, how you see who's doing the taking and hoarding, and how you figure out who the real aggressors are in international conflicts.

2. The three most overlooked and under-appreciated aspects of the human experience are consciousness, the extent to which conditioned thought patterns dictate our lives, and the influence of propaganda.

3. We live in a civilization that's so pervasively steeped in lies and manipulations that the only way to have a truth-based relationship with reality is to drop all your assumptions and premises about what's true and begin examining everything from the very beginning with fresh eyes.

4. The phenomenon known as spiritual enlightenment is a real thing which we are all capable of realizing, and the fact that this potential exists within our species has many far-reaching implications for what we are capable of attaining as a civilization.

5. Everything is beautiful. Not seeing the beauty in something is always the failure of the perceiver, not the thing being perceived.

6. Happiness is the natural default position of human consciousness. It's only through egoic delusions that we trick ourselves into unhappiness.

7. There are strange untapped potentials within our species which our philosophies don't touch on, our religions don't anticipate, our academia doesn't acknowledge, and our common worldviews don't account for.

8. Reality is nondual. There's no real separation between the perceiver and that which is perceived, or between any of the objects in sense perception. All is indivisible.

9. The self is an illusion held together by believed mental narratives and fear-based energetic fixations. This illusion can be seen through and transcended.

10. It's possible for two people to keep falling more and more deeply in love with each other for their entire lives, as long as they're both intensely curious about each other and both keep growing and discovering new parts of themselves to love.

11. The feeling of guilt is useless and can safely be dropped entirely. The only people who might benefit from feeling some guilt are the sociopaths and psychopaths among us who never experience it anyway. For those among us with healthy empathy centers, guilt is unnecessary to motivate good behavior and often becomes a tool that manipulators use to control us.

12. Antisocial personality disorder, more commonly known as sociopathy and psychopathy, is one of the greatest obstacles to human thriving. That there really are creatures among us who don't think or feel like the rest of us do and frequently use their lack of empathy to climb the ladders of wealth and power sounds made up (and even sounds like the basis of many racist belief systems), but it is a fact. Not until our species becomes so emotionally intelligent and awake that sociopaths and psychopaths are unable to thrive in it or go unseen will this problem disappear.

13. You can recognize sociopaths, psychopaths, and other narcissists in your life by paying attention to how much energy they pour into convincing you to believe stories about others, about themselves, and especially about you. Someone who often spends energy trying to get you to believe negative things about yourself is someone you should get out of your life as quickly as possible.

14. There really is a struggle in our world between light and darkness, though it doesn't look how the movies tell us to expect it. Those in power seek to keep their dark deeds hidden in darkness by maintaining government secrecy, propaganda and censorship. The manipulators in our own lives seek to keep their manipulations and misdeeds hidden in the same way. Even within our own personal psychology there are dysfunctional structures which seek to remain hidden in the unconscious. Humanity's struggle is to bring that all into the light.

15. A sincere devotion to knowing the truth is the path toward happiness, health and harmony, for humans as individuals and for humanity as a collective. Knowing what's true about ourselves uncovers our inner dysfunctionality and leads to healing and enlightenment. Knowing what's true about our world leads to an understanding of the abusive nature of our power structures and societal systems. Continually striving toward the light of truth will bring us all home.

Image via Adobe Stock

The Star-Spangled Kangaroo

A new US warship has been ushered into service in Sydney. The ship is called the USS Canberra to honor the military union of the United States and Australia, and, if that's still too subtle for you, it has a literal star-spangled kangaroo affixed to its side.

That's right: the first US warship ever commissioned in a foreign port has been emblazoned with a kangaroo covered in the stars and stripes of the United States flag. An Australian officer will reportedly always be part of the staff of the ship, to further symbolize the holy matrimony between Australia and the US war machine.

"I can think of no better symbol of this shared future than the USS Canberra," gushed US ambassador to Australia Caroline Kennedy. "Built by American workers at an Australian company in Mobile, Alabama, her crew will always include a Royal Australian Navy sailor, and from today forward, she will proudly display a star-spangled kangaroo."

And you know what? She's right. Not because of her giddy joy over the complete absorption of Australia into the US military apparatus of course—that's a horrifying nightmare which is increasingly putting this nation on track toward a frontline role in Washington's war plans against China. But she's right that the star-spangled kangaroo and the ship which carries it is a perfect symbol for the way these two nations have become inseparably intertwined.

In fact, I'd take it a step further. I'd say the star-spangled kangaroo should be the new symbol for our entire nation.

I mean, we might as well, right? Australia is not a sovereign nation in any meaningful way; we're functionally a US military/intelligence asset, and according to our defence minister Richard Marles our own military is being moved "beyond interoperability to interchangeability" with the US war machine so they can "operate seamlessly together, at speed."

The US imprisons Australian journalist Julian Assange for exposing US war crimes like he's the personal property of the Pentagon, and when the US doesn't like our Prime Minister because he's too keen on Australian independence or perceived as too friendly with China, they simply replace him with another one.

We even found out recently that Australians are not permitted to know if the US is bringing nuclear weapons into this country. That is a secret the US keeps from all of us, and our government respects their privacy on the matter.

So I think the star-spangled kangaroo is an entirely appropriate symbol for this country. Put it on our flag. Put it on our money. Put it on all our warships and planes, and on every military uniform. When you walk into an Australian government building, Yankarooey (or whatever stupid Aussie nickname we make up for the thing to mask our own cognitive dissonance) should be the first thing everyone sees.

Undignified? Certainly. Humiliating? Absolutely. An admission that Australia is not a real nation? Of course. But at least it would be honest. If we're going to act like Washington's subservient basement gimp, we may as well dress the part.

Image via Department of Defense

More Warmongers Elevated In The Biden Administration

The Biden administration looks set to become even more warlike than it already was if you can imagine, with virulent Russia hawk Victoria Nuland and virulent China hawk Charles Q Brown now being elevated to lofty positions by the White House.

Nuland, the wife of alpha neocon Robert Kagan, has been named acting deputy secretary of state by President Biden, at least until a new deputy secretary has been named. This places her at second in command within the State Department, second only to Tony Blinken.

In an article about Nuland's unique role in souring relations between the US and Russia during her previous tenure in the State Department under Obama, Responsible Statecraft's Connor Echols writes the following of the latest news:

Nuland's appointment will be a boon for Russia hawks who want to turn up the heat on the Kremlin. But, for those who favor a negotiated end to the conflict in Ukraine, a promotion for the notoriously "undiplomatic diplomat" will be a bitter pill.

A few quick reminders are in order. When Nuland was serving in the Obama administration, she had a now-infamous leaked call with the U.S. ambassador to Ukraine. As the Maidan Uprising roiled the country, the pair of American diplomats discussed conversations with opposition leaders, and Nuland expressed support for putting Arseniy Yatseniuk into power. (Yatseniuk would become prime minister later that month, after Russia-friendly

former President Viktor Yanukovych fled the country.) At one memorable point in the call, Nuland said "Fu–k the EU" in response to Europe's softer stance on the protests.

The controversy surrounding the call—and larger implications of U.S. involvement in the ouster of Yanukovych—kicked up tensions with Russia and contributed to Russian President Vladimir Putin's decision to seize Crimea and support an insurgency in eastern Ukraine. Her handing out food to demonstrators on the ground in Kyiv probably didn't help either. Nuland, along with State Department sanctions czar Daniel Fried, then led the effort to punish Putin through sanctions. Another official at State reportedly asked Fried if "the Russians realize that the two hardest-line people in the entire U.S. government are now in a position to go after them?"

In a 2015 Consortium News article titled "The Mess That Nuland Made," the late Robert Parry singled out Nuland as the primary architect of the 2014 regime change operation in Ukraine, which, as Aaron Maté explained last year, paved the way to the war we're seeing there today. Hopefully her position winds up being temporary.

In other news, the Senate Arms Services Committee has voted to confirm Biden's selection of General Charles Q Brown Jr as the next chairman of the Joint Chiefs of Staff, replacing Mark Milley. A full senate vote will now take place on whether to confirm Brown—currently the Air Force Chief of Staff—for the nation's highest military office.

Brown is unambiguous about his belief that the US must hasten to militarize against China in the so-called Indo-Pacific to prepare for confrontation between the two powers, calling for more US bases in the region and increased efforts to arm Taiwan during his hearing before the Senate Arms Services Committee earlier this month.

Back in May, Moon of Alabama flagged Brown's nomination in an article which also noted that several advocates of military restraint had been resigning from their positions within the administration, including Wendy Sherman, the deputy secretary of state who Nuland has taken over for.

It's too soon to draw any firm conclusions, but to see voices of restraint stepping down and proponents of escalation stepping up could be a bad portent of things to come.

·

The Empire Knows It's Pouring Ukrainian Blood Into An Unwinnable Proxy War

In an article titled "Ukraine's Lack of Weaponry and Training Risks Stalemate in Fight With Russia," The Wall Street Journal's Daniel Michaels reports that western officials knew Ukrainian forces didn't have the weapons and training necessary to succeed in their highly touted counteroffensive which was launched last month.

Michaels writes:

"When Ukraine launched its big counteroffensive this spring, Western military officials knew Kyiv didn't have all the training or weapons—from shells to warplanes—that it needed to dislodge Russian forces. But they hoped Ukrainian courage and resourcefulness would carry the day.

"They haven't. Deep and deadly minefields, extensive fortifications and Russian air power have combined to largely block significant advances by Ukrainian troops. Instead, the campaign risks descending into a stalemate with the potential to burn through lives and equipment without a major shift in momentum."

The claim that western officials had sincerely believed Ukrainian forces might be able to overcome their glaring deficits through sheer pluck and ticker is undermined later in the same article by a war pundit who says the US would never attempt such a counteroffensive without first controlling the skies, which Ukraine doesn't have the ability to do:

"America would never attempt to defeat a prepared defense without air superiority, but they [Ukrainians] don't have air superiority," the U.S. Army War College's John Nagl told WSJ. *"It's impossible to overstate how important air superiority is for fighting a ground fight at a reasonable cost in casualties."*

Antiwar's Dave DeCamp writes the following on the latest WSJ revelation:

"Leading up to the Ukrainian counteroffensive, which was launched in June, the Discord leaks and media reports revealed that

the US did not believe Ukraine could regain much territory from Russia. But the Biden administration pushed for the assault anyway, as it rejected the idea of a pause in fighting."

So the empire is still knowingly throwing Ukrainian lives into the meat grinder of an unwinnable proxy war, even as western officials tell the public that this war is about saving Ukrainian lives and handing Putin a crushing defeat whenever they're on camera.

This attitude from the empire is not a new development. Last October The Washington Post reported that "Privately, U.S. officials say neither Russia nor Ukraine is capable of winning the war outright, but they have ruled out the idea of pushing or even nudging Ukraine to the negotiating table."

Now why might that be? Why would the western empire be so comfortable encouraging Ukrainians to keep fighting when it knows they can't win?

We find our answer in another Washington Post article titled "The West feels gloomy about Ukraine. Here's why it shouldn't.", authored by virulent empire propagandist David Ignatius. In his eagerness to frame the floundering counteroffensive in a positive light for his American audience, Ignatius let slip an inconvenient truth:

"Meanwhile, for the United States and its NATO allies, these 18 months of war have been a strategic windfall, at relatively low cost (other than for the Ukrainians). The West's most reckless antagonist has been rocked. NATO has grown much stronger with the additions of Sweden and Finland.

Germany has weaned itself from dependence on Russian energy and, in many ways, rediscovered its sense of values. NATO squabbles make headlines, but overall, this has been a triumphal summer for the alliance."

Anyone who believes this proxy war is about helping Ukrainians should be made to read that paragraph over and over again until it sinks in. The admission that the US-centralized power structure benefits immensely from this proxy conflict is revealing enough, but that parenthetical "other than for the Ukrainians" aside really drives it home. It reads as though it was added as an afterthought, like "Oh yeah it's actually kind of rough on the Ukrainians though—if you consider them to be people."

The claim that this war is about helping Ukrainians has been further undermined by another new Washington Post report that Ukraine is now more riddled with land mines than any other nation on earth, and that US-supplied cluster munitions are only making the land more deadly.

That's right kids! We're turning Ukraine into an uninhabitable wasteland of death and dismemberment to save the Ukrainians.

We should probably talk more about the fact that the US empire is loudly promoting the goal of achieving peace in Ukraine by defeating Russia while quietly acknowledging that this goal is impossible. This is like accelerating toward a brick wall and pretending it's an open road.

The narrative that Russia can be beaten by ramping up proxy warfare against it makes sense if you believe Russia can be militarily defeated in

Ukraine, but the US empire does not believe that Russia can be militarily defeated in Ukraine. It knows that continuing this war is only going to perpetuate the death and devastation.

"Beat Putin's ass and make him withdraw" sounds cool and is egoically gratifying, and it's become the mainstream answer to the problem of the war in Ukraine, but nobody promoting that answer can address the fact that the ones driving this proxy war believe it's impossible. In fact, all evidence we're seeing suggests that the US is not trying to deliver Putin a crushing defeat in Ukraine and force him to withdraw, but is rather trying to create another long and costly military quagmire for Moscow, as western cold warriors have done repeatedly in instances like Afghanistan and Syria.

Wanting to weaken Russia and wanting to save lives and establish peace in Ukraine are two completely different goals, so different that in practice they wind up being largely contradictory. Drawing Moscow into a bloody quagmire means many more people dying in a war that drags on for years, with all the immense human suffering that that entails.

The US does not want peace in Ukraine, it wants to overextend Russia, shore up military and energy dominance over Europe, expand its war machine and enrich the military-industrial complex. That's why it knowingly provoked this war. It's posing as Ukraine's savior while being clearly invested in Ukraine's destruction.

It is not legitimate to support this proxy war without squarely addressing this massive contradiction using hard facts and robust argumentation. Nobody ever has.

Image via Adobe Stock

Disrupt The Culture Wars

One of the great challenges faced by westerners who oppose the political status quo today is the way the narrative managers of both mainstream factions continuously divert all political energy away from issues which threaten the interests of the powerful like economic injustice, war, militarism, authoritarianism, corruption, capitalism and ecocide and toward issues which don't threaten the powerful at all like abortion, racism, sexism, homophobia and transphobia.

This method of social control serves the powerful in some very obvious ways, and is being used very effectively. As long as it remains effective, it will continue to be used. The worse things get the more urgent the need to fight the class war will become, anf the more urgent the need to fight the class war becomes the more vitriolic and intense the artificial culture war will become in order to prevent political changes which inconvenience the powerful. This is 100 percent guaranteed. And what's tricky is that all the vitriolic intensity will create the illusion that the *culture war* has gotten more important, when in reality the *class war* has.

It's just a straightforward fact that the more miserable, impoverished and disempowered the public becomes, the more hateful and all-consuming the artificial culture war will be made to prevent revolution. That's what's been happening, and that's what will continue to happen. You can hate hearing it, and you can hate me for saying it. But it is a fact, and I think we all pretty much know it's a fact.

So what's do be done about this? Obviously it's not an option to just throw disempowered groups to the wolves and ignore the abuses they're suffering under the directed hatred coming after them from the right. And obviously it's not an option to run to the other side of the artificial partisan divide and play along with the mainstream faction which says we should focus **only** on culture war issues, as in Hillary Clinton famously arguing that breaking up the banks won't end racism and sexism.

As with most problems, the first step toward finding a solution is to bring consciousness to what's happening. Draw attention to the fact that marginalized groups are being used and abused by mainstream narrative managers to keep the public from turning their gaze on the abuses of their rulers. Draw attention to the way rightist narrative managers direct hatred toward marginalized groups to keep hatred away from our rulers, **and** to the way liberal narrative managers seize on that to direct their herd away from issues that can inconvenience the powerful and toward exclusive focus on the culture war.

Stop letting people get sucked up into the performance, and instead draw attention to what's really going on here. Act like a loud jerk at a movie theater who keeps yelling "None of this is real! Those are actors on a movie set!"

Can you imagine how hard it would be to get lost in the narrative of a movie if somebody was constantly doing that to you? After a while you'd stop seeing Oppenheimer and you'd only be able to see Cillian Murphy.

Basically all you're trying to do is take all the emotional heat that's being diverted into partisan feuding over issues whose outcomes will never inconvenience power in the slightest, and stear that emotional heat toward the people who are directing all this. This is both easy to do and completely honest, because how fucked up is it that they're doing this? How fucked up is it that the most influential voices in our society on both sides of the mainstream partisan divide are facilitating the abuse of marginalized groups in order to protect the powerful?

It's about as loathsome a thing as you could possibly come up with. They're pitting human against human at the expense of society's most vulnerable members and watching them fight from on high like Greek gods. Can you think of anything more vile?

Draw attention to how disgusting what they're doing is. Draw attention to how deeply evil this behavior is. Keep shouting in that movie theater and drawing attention to what's really going on to highlight how profoundly depraved these monsters really are.

Draw people's attention to this dynamic wherever you see it. When right wing "populists" babble about LGBTQ conspiracies and shriek about wokeness, mock them for the ridiculous sheep they are for playing into a dynamic that directly serves the elite power structures they claim to oppose. When liberals are ignoring economic injustice, war, militarism, authoritarianism, corruption, capitalism and ecocide to focus on culture war battles whose outcomes will never even slightly inconvenience the powerful, highlight the disgusting way they themselves are feeding into a dynamic that imperils the marginalized communities they claim to defend.

People on both sides of the divide will object to this message. The source of their objection is the exact programming I just described. The truth hides just beneath that objection. On some level you all know this is happening.

Keep breaking the spell and drawing attention to what's really going on, and you can stomp out the abuse at its source.

Image via Adobe Stock

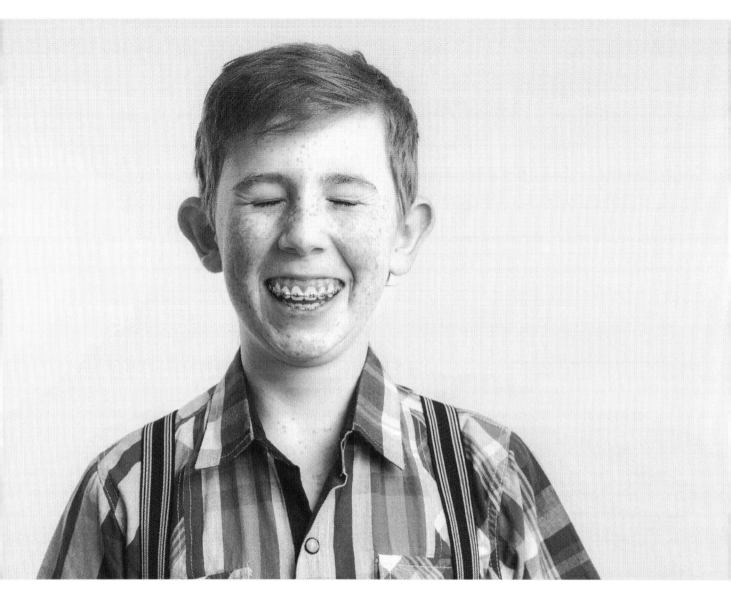

We're Just A Confused Species In An Awkward Transition Phase

Really, when it comes right down to it, things are a mess because humans are in a very awkward and confusing stage in our development as a species.

Our giant brains evolved faster than we could adjust to, and now we're these scared little apex predators stumbling around the earth with massive prefrontal cortices overlaying a bunch of deep primordial conditioning. A rapidly developed capacity for language and abstract thought strapped on top of a fear response that our distant evolutionary ancestors developed to help them run away from long-extinct monsters with big sharp teeth.

This sudden change has left us in a transition stage where we haven't yet gotten the hang of the immense power which now erupts from within our skulls and gives us the ability to shape our world to our will. Like how the ancient mammalian ancestors of whales probably looked awkward when they first began reentering the sea, before they got the hang of swimming and their nostrils moved to a location more conducive to breathing in the water.

It's left us at this weird, uncomfortable stage where we have the intelligence to do amazing things, but haven't yet developed the wisdom to use this newfound capacity in a harmonious way.

We now have the ability to conquer our own ecosystems using technology, but we lack the wisdom not to do so.

We have the intelligence to invent nuclear weapons, but we lack the wisdom not to build them.

We have the ability to plan for our individual futures, but we lack the wisdom to make sure our species as a whole has a future.

We have the ability to think abstract thoughts, but lack the wisdom to refrain from building identities out of them.

We have the ability to ask questions, but lack the wisdom to deeply question our own true nature and whether the world is really as it seems.

The ability to write vast tomes of philosophy that contain not one line telling us how to be content on the planet we were born on.

The ability to construct entire belief systems that are completely useless for learning to live in harmony with what is.

The ability to discover spirituality only to use it for vapid escapism and tyrannical psychological domination.

The ability to research human psychology only to use it to convince people to buy junk they don't need and support wars they don't want and vote for politicians they don't like.

The ability to invent mass media only to use use it to promote and normalize a status quo that is killing us all.

The ability to invent something as transcendental as music only to popularize songs about owning stuff and getting money.

The ability to technologically link billions of minds on the internet only to spend all our time arguing about nonsense.

The ability to tell stories only to spend our energy using storytelling to manipulate and control each other.

The ability to intimately appreciate beauty and mystery with a profound depth and complexity only to spend our entire lives frantically doing anything but that.

We have the ability to do all these things skillfully and harmoniously; we just haven't quite gotten the hang of it yet.

It's like when you got your first bike for your birthday and you knew it could make you go a lot faster than you normally can, but it took a lot of practice before you went from training wheels and painful falls to swiftly breezing through the neighborhood. These giant prefrontal cortices we got on our birthday give us so much potential, and we've been bumbling around on training wheels and taking nasty spills when we try to take them off.

I'm sure the early evolutionary ancestors of birds were awkward as hell too before they finally got the hang of flying. They would have looked ridiculous, and it wouldn't have been immediately clear from an outsider's perspective exactly what nature was going for there. Like biological baby scribbles.

The only difference is that the awkward evolutionary transition phases of birds and whales did not involve giant neural networks which make childbirth painful and could easily lead to the death of all terrestrial life.

The birth of a human baby is difficult due to the size of our enormous, rapidly evolved brains relative to our more slowly evolved pelvic bones. The birth of a sane humanity will be difficult for similar reasons.

I do believe we have the ability to make the jump from this awkward transition phase to become a truly conscious species. But it looks like if we do make it, it's going to be by the skin of our omnivore teeth.

Image via Adobe Stock

Ideas For A Dystopian Novel

I've been kicking around some ideas for a dystopian novel lately, and I was hoping readers might be able to provide me with some feedback.

I'm picturing a story set in a world where everyone's a slave but doesn't know it. People think thoughts they believe they came up with themselves, make decisions and lifestyle choices that they think are their own, buy things they sincerely believe they want, consume entertainment they honestly feel they enjoy, vote for political candidates they truly think they support, when in reality they're all marching in complete obedience to an elite ruling class whose high-level mastery of mass-scale psychological manipulation has bent the public to their will.

In my novel people will be funneled from early childhood through an education system designed by plutocrats and social engineers to create efficient and compliant gear-turners, then when they are grown their programming continues in the form of mass media indoctrination. If they become politically aware they are funneled into artificially constructed ideological perspectives that are designed to look truthful and appealing but which don't challenge existing power structures in any meaningful way.

In the same way, the political system in this dark alternate reality is designed to look free and democratic, but there's no real connection between how people vote and the way their civilization actually functions. An unacknowledged, unofficial alliance of plutocrats and government operatives makes the actual decisions about how money, industry, government, and military forces will behave from day to day, and this secretive alliance controls the official political system the public believes is responsible for overseeing those matters. What people call "elections" are actually just the public choosing between two lackeys of that ruling alliance, and their only meaningful disagreements are on how the will of those rulers should best be advanced.

My dystopian society is built on endless violence, oppression and exploitation, but because in this world the science of mass-scale psychological manipulation is so advanced, people don't even know that it's happening. Mass murder is committed continuously in nonstop military operations overseas, and the public is successfully convinced that it's to promote freedom and democracy and keep them safe from terrorism. People have to work multiple jobs in the wealthiest nation in the world just to put food on the table, and they are brainwashed into believing it's their fault for not making better life choices. People die of exposure on the streets while billionaires rake in exponentially more wealth, and the public is programmed to believe it's because the latter work harder than the former. Police forces and prison systems keep expanding in order to exert more control and people are trained to believe it's to make them safe from crime. Journalists are imprisoned for telling the truth and people are told it's to protect national security. Information on the internet is aggressively controlled and people

are propagandized into accepting that it's to protect them from dangerous speech.

In my dystopian novel the powerful will simply do as they please and then promote narratives to explain why those actions were justified. If a smaller, weaker government isn't sufficiently obedient to the world's dominant power structure, reasons will be manufactured to explain why they must be ousted. If it's necessary to exert more control at home or abroad, justifications will emerge for why military expansionism is needed in this or that geostrategically important region or why increased domestic surveillance is required to keep people safe. The armed goons and war machines move wherever they are needed, and the public is either kept in the dark about those movements or told made-up stories explaining why they must occur.

Endless mass military slaughter is essential for the existence of the ruling power structure in this dystopia, because without it the world's governments would simply behave in whatever way advances their own interests. The government is so profoundly corrupt that the corporations who manufacture military weaponry are inseparably intertwined with the decision-making apparatus of its foreign policy establishment and are permitted to actively lobby for more wars so that more of its expensive weaponry will be used. Mountains of human corpses are amassed for no other reason than because it is more profitable to launch weapons at them than to leave them alone. Nuclear weapons are stockpiled and placed around the world for no other reason than because it is profitable to make more of them.

It's the same with environmental and economic policies. A global system is held in place at gunpoint in which

mass-scale human behavior is driven by the pursuit of profit for its own sake, so environmental and economic policies just like military policies are formed not based on what would be best but on what would be most profitable for the plutocrats who shape those policies. Industry moves in whatever way rakes in the most money, no matter who it hurts, no matter how badly it imperils humanity.

And everyone just marches along with it, because they are manipulated into accepting this disaster by sophisticated propaganda systems, by movies and TV shows designed to normalize the dystopia they exist in, by tightly controlled information access, and by their own psychological compartmentalization since the reality of their situation is too disturbing to look at directly. They turn the gears of their dark world and then stay up late binging on soulless comedy shows to distract them from the horrors lurking just beneath the surface.

Obviously such a dystopia would be completely unsustainable and the most obvious ending would be to kill the whole world off within a few books by nuclear war or ecological disaster or something equally terrible, but maybe I could have the populace simply wake up to the manipulations and take back their will and shrug off the elites' control like a warm coat on a summer's day? I dunno. Something tells me that for some unknown reason today's readers are too inured with learned helplessness and knee-jerk pessimism to be able to even imagine such a scenario, let alone accept it as a believable development.

Anyway, that's my pitch. What do you all think? Does this thing have legs? Or is it too different from today's world for people to relate to?

Image via Adobe Stock

A Helpful Suggestion

Headlines in the 2020s are continually dominated by the US proxy war against Russia in Ukraine and US brinkmanship against China with Taiwan.

The US asserts that it has been well within its rights to bring NATO to Russia's doorstep and convert Ukraine into a heavily-armed NATO asset, and that it is perfectly entitled to menace China with military encirclement and its provocations with Taiwan. When Russia and China contend that these actions pose a threat to their national security interests, US empire managers argue that no nation is entitled to a "sphere of influence" beyond their own territory, and that the US is just helping its good friends on the borders of its top two geopolitical rivals protect themselves.

If I may, I have a solution that could help the US defend its foreign policy a bit more convincingly: simply welcome Russia and China to amass military forces in Latin America.

If the US made it clear that it would do nothing to prevent Russia and China from militarizing the nations south of the US border to the furthest extent possible, after those military presences begin to appear empire critics will no longer be able to claim that the US is the clear and obvious aggressor in its conflicts with Moscow and Beijing.

This would entail officially abolishing longstanding policies like the Monroe Doctrine and the Roosevelt Corollary thereto which have led to the US continually intervening in Latin American affairs to crush socialism and advance its own interests, often with extreme violence and to the great detriment of the people who live there. Once the US has made it clear that Russia and China have an open path to establish an extensive military presence in Latin America using the same means the US has used to establish its military presence in eastern Europe and eastern Asia, opponents of Washington's foreign policy will soon lose the ability to accuse the US empire of flagrant hypocrisy.

Let China militarize as much as it wants in socialist countries like Cuba, Venezuela, Nicaragua and Bolivia. Let Russia make some military deals with Mexico and Brazil. Let them patrol their warships along the east and west coastline of the United States, and hang out in the Gulf of Mexico for as long as they like. Let them build bases. Let them build missile systems. Let them set up anything they like using whatever means they can get away with in the nations in that region, because according to the United States that's all perfectly fine.

Then the US will have legitimacy in the arguments it has been making about its militarization around Russia and China. Then the objections from Moscow and Beijing to that militarization can legitimately be framed as unreasonable. Because the rules will be applied equally to all parties.

Of course, we all know this will never happen. If Russia or China began amassing military threats to US regional dominance in Latin America, it would immediately be treated as an act of war. The last time a foreign power placed a military threat to the United States near its coastline, it was responded to so aggressively that the world almost ended.

This is because the "rules" in the US empire's much-touted "rules-based international order" do not apply to the US empire. They're the for-thee-but-not-for-me kind of rules.

The drivers of the empire truly believe that the entire planet is their property, and that anyone who resists this claim is essentially attacking the United States. Its planetary hegemony is treated as the baseline norm, and any opposition to it is treated as a freakish affront to freedom and democracy.

The US empire claims to use its domination of the world stage to uphold the world order, yet it can only continue to dominate the world stage by endless violence, chaos and disorder. The US is the clear aggressor in its confrontations with Russia and China. It is an insatiable monster who feeds on human blood, and world peace will never be possible as long as it rules over us.

Image via Pixabay

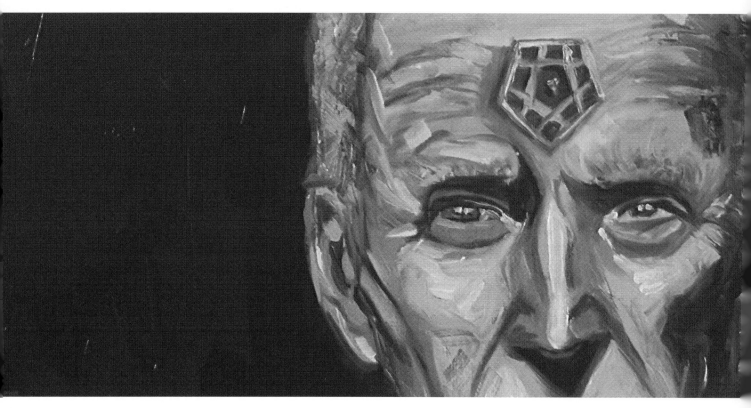

The True Symbol Of The United States Is The Pentagon

The real symbol of the United States is not the stars and stripes, nor the bald eagle, nor the Statue of Liberty, nor even the mighty McDonald's logo. The real symbol of the United States is the Pentagon.

The Pentagon should feature centrally on the US flag. It should be on the coins and on all the bills, and it should appear next to the name of every American in the Olympics. When anyone sees a five-sided polygon, they should immediately think "United States of America".

There is nothing more representative of the most significant things about the United States than the Pentagon. Sure the US has lovely national parks, an abundance of fast food chains and 500 million-dollar superhero movies, but nothing has anywhere near the effect on the world as the US government's ability to project force around the planet with military violence and the threat thereof.

That is the main thing that makes the US unique among nations, after all. Americans are taught from childhood to take special pride in their nation's "freedom" and "democracy" (of which they have neither), when what actually makes their country stand out against the crowd is its role as the hub of a globe-spanning empire that is held together by nonstop military aggression. The five-sided building which houses the US Department of Defense—formerly called the Department of War until someone noticed that was a bit too truthful—is the perfect symbol for that empire. It conveys what the United States is really putting out into the world more accurately than any other.

It's easy to forget that you live in the hub of the most powerful empire in history when you actually live there, in the same way it's so calm in the eye of a hurricane that you'd hardly know your world is being ripped apart around you. But because the US-centralized empire influences global dynamics so pervasively, and because every major international conflict in the world involves it to some degree, that's what affects the most people in the world to the furthest extent right now. How much money they have. Whether they get to feed their kids today. Whether they'll be torn to shreds by military explosives tomorrow. Whether they'll have to watch everyone die in a nuclear holocaust next year.

So as far as humanity is concerned the most distinctive thing about the United States is its empire, and the most accurate symbol for that empire is the Pentagon. Artists, activists and memesters should make more use of this powerful symbol, because it's right there, easy to draw and everything.

Mainstream Journalists Are Cloistered Ivy League–Educated Trust Fund Kids

Iraq war cheerleader David Brooks has an article in The New York Times titled "What if We're the Bad Guys Here?", another one of those tired old think pieces we've been seeing for the last eight years that asks "golly gosh could we coastal elites have played some role in the rise of Trumpism?" like it's the first time anyone has ever considered that obvious point (the answer is yes, duh, you soft-handed silver spoon-fed ivory tower bubble boy).

One worthwhile paragraph about the media stands out though:

"Over the last decades we've taken over whole professions and locked everybody else out. When I began my journalism career in Chicago in the 1980s, there were still some old crusty working-class guys around the newsroom. Now we're not only a college-dominated profession, we're an elite-college-dominated profession. Only 0.8 percent of all college students graduate from the super elite 12 schools (the Ivy League colleges, plus Stanford, M.I.T., Duke and the University of Chicago). A 2018 study found that more than 50 percent of the staff writers at the beloved New York Times and The Wall Street Journal attended one of the 29 most elite universities in the nation."

Brooks is not the first commentator to make this observation about the drastic shift in the socioeconomic makeup of news reporters that has taken place from previous generations to now.

"The class factor in journalism gets overlooked," journalist Glenn Greenwald said on the Jimmy Dore Show in 2021. "Thirty or forty years ago, fifty years ago, journalists really were outsiders. That's why they all had unions; they made shit money, they came from like working class families. They hated the elite. They hated bankers and politicians. It was kind of like a boss-employee relationship—they hated them and wanted to throw rocks at them and take them down pegs."

"If I were to list the twenty richest people I've ever met in my entire life, I think like seven or eight of them are people I met because they work at The Intercept—people from like the richest fucking families on the planet," Greenwald added.

Journalist Matt Taibbi, whose father worked for NBC, made similar observations on the Dark Horse podcast back in 2020.

"Reporters when I was growing up, they came from a different class of people than they do today," Taibbi said. "A lot of them were kind of more working class—their parents were more likely to be plumbers or electricians than they were to be doctors or lawyers. Like this thing where the journalist is an Ivy League grad, that's a relatively new thing that I think came about in the seventies and eighties with my generation. But reporters just instinctively hated rich people, they hated powerful people. Like if you put up a poster of a politician in a newsroom it was defaced instantaneously, like there were darts on it. Reporters saw it as their job to stick it to the man."

"Mostly the job is different now," Taibbi said. "The fantasy among reporters in the nineties about politicians started to be, I want to be the person that hangs out with the candidate after the speech and has a beer and is sort of close to power. And that's kind of the model, that's where we're at right now. That's kind of the problem is that basically people in the business want to be behind the rope line with people of influence. And it's going to be a problem to get us back to that other adversarial posture of the past."

This is a major reason behind the freakish sycophancy and empire loyalism we see in the mainstream press. It's not just the obscenely wealthy owners of the mass media who are protecting their class interests — it's the reporters, editors and pundits as well.

These are typically fairly wealthy people from fairly wealthy families, who become more and more wealthy the more their careers are elevated. As insiders of the mainstream press have attested, it's widely understood by employees of the mainstream media that the way to elevate your career is to toe the establishment line and refrain from spotlighting issues that are inconvenient to the powerful.

This identification with the ruling class feeds into the dynamic described by Taibbi in which modern journalists have come to value close proximity to those in power. These are the people they want to be sharing drinks with and going to parties with and invited to the weddings of; the "us vs them" dynamic which used to exist between the press and politicians switched, and now the press see themselves and the politicians they fraternize with as "us" and the general public as "them".

There are other factors at play with regard to elite education. The number of journalists with college degrees skyrocketed from 58 percent in 1971 to 92 percent in 2013; if your wealthy parents aren't paying that off for you then you've got crushing student debt that you need to pay off yourself, which you can only do in the field you studied in by making a decent amount of money, which you can only do by acting as a dependable propagandist for the imperial establishment.

Universities themselves tend to play a status quo-serving, conformity-manufacturing role when churning out journalists, as wealth won't flow into an academic environment that

is offensive to the wealthy. Moneyed interests are unlikely to make large donations to universities which teach their students that moneyed interests are a plague upon the nation, and they are certainly not going to send their kids there.

"The whole intellectual culture has a filtering system, starting as a child in school," Noam Chomsky once explained in an interview. "You're expected to accept certain beliefs, styles, behavioral patterns and so on. If you don't accept them, you are called maybe a behavioral problem, or something, and you're weeded out. Something like that goes on all the way through universities and graduate schools. There is an implicit system of filtering... which creates a strong tendency to impose conformism."

The people who make it through this filtering system are the ones who are elevated to the most influential positions in our civilization. All the most widely amplified voices in our society are the celebrities, journalists, pundits and politicians who've proven themselves to be reliable stewards of the matrix of narrative control which keeps the public jacked in to the mainstream worldview.

Is it any wonder, then, that all the sources we've been taught to look to for information about our world continually feed us stories which give the impression that the status quo is working fine and this is the only way things can possibly be? Is it any wonder that the mass media support all US wars and cheerlead all imperial agendas?

This is how things were set up to be. Our media act like propagandists for a tyrannical regime because that's exactly what they are.

Image via Adobe Stock

The Boy And The Starfish And The Yawning Chasm Of Infinity

A man walking along the beach came upon a boy picking up starfish and throwing them into the water.

"What are you doing?" the man asked him.

"I'm throwing these starfish back into the sea," the boy answered. "The tide's gone out and they'll cook in the sun if I don't help them."

"But there are miles and miles of beach and countless starfish in every mile," said the man. "You can't possibly make any difference!"

The boy listened politely, then picked up another starfish and tossed it into the surf.

"Made a difference to that one," he said to the man.

"I mean that's a cute answer and all," said the man. "It would fit nicely in a Facebook meme shared by your religious aunty, or a motivational speech from the early nineties. But in the grand scheme of things you must surely understand that saving that one starfish is of no real significance? The tide will go out again tomorrow, and this beach will once again be lined with dying starfish just as it is now, among them quite likely our little friend you just rescued."

"What do you want me to say man?" the boy replied, his tone suddenly changing. "That there's some kind of eternally ordained metaphysical justification for my actions here on this beach today? That there's some absolute truth inscribed upon the fabric of reality from on high saying 'One saved starfish equals one Ultimate Meaningfulness?' On what basis are you premising your assumption that any actions have any meaning or purpose at all?"

"I- I- Well..." the man stammered.

The boy began to grow larger, and as he spoke his skin turned an otherworldly shade of blue.

"Do you have any idea how vast the universe is? How ancient it is? How ephemeral it is?" asked the boy. "How can you claim to take any action that makes any ultimate difference whatsoever when you and everything you've ever known is nothing but an infinitely small blip in the middle of a yawning expanse of infinity?"

"Who- who are you?" the man asked.

A second pair of blue arms sprouted from the boy's torso. His voice thundered as he towered over the man.

"Who am I?? Who are you?" the boy responded. "Who do you think you are exactly? Who are you to go around proclaiming what actions possess significance and which do not? You've been around, what? Sixty years? You're a zygote. You're a fruit fly. The very thing you think of as yourself is no more substantial than a wisp of sea foam, and as far as the universe is concerned you have essentially the same lifespan. You're nothing but a loosely associated cloud of cells swirling around for a short time in inseparable interplay with the ecosystem which birthed it on a tiny planet in the outer periphery of a galaxy which in the grand scheme of things is scarcely older than you are. You're a little eddie twirling in the middle of the ocean for a single instant, and you presume yourself so wise and authoritative that you can pass out decrees on the meaningfulness of the life of a starfish? You presume yourself any more important or significant than any one of these starfish on the sand?"

"I'm sorry!" the man said, falling to his knees in terror. "I meant no offense!"

The world fell away as the boy's hulking frame came apart and transformed into billions of galaxies spinning against a backdrop of infinite blackness.

"The universe expands and contracts within me like the air in your lungs," the boy said. "Each Big Bang in every universe unleashes a new dance of swirling energy which turns into increasingly complex iterations of matter as it expands, it achieves peaks of dazzling beauty the likes of which your young primate mind cannot even imagine, then it grows cold and collapses in on itself once again. Again and again I birth infinite universes into existence; they bloom and die within me like flowers in the illusory appearance of time. Not one of those universes ever matters. Not one of them ever makes any ultimate difference. The life of a single starfish has the same net worth as the entire lifespan of this entire universe."

"Then why bother?" asked the man, suddenly finding some courage. "If nothing means anything and nothing matters, why create any of this?"

"Same reason I sometimes throw starfish back into the ocean," said the boy.

"Which is what?"

"You were married, yes?" the boy asked in response.

"Yes," said the man, taken aback. "She died recently."

"Did you love her?"

"Yes. Very much."

"Ever tell her so?"

"Yes. Many times."

"Ever do nice things for her?"

"Yes."

"Why?"

"Why... because I loved her. There was no other reason."

"Yeah, well, same here."

"You love all these universes you create?"

"Immensely."

"Then why do you let them die? Why do you let them be imperfect? Motherfucker, why do you let cancer exist??"

"That's not how love works, man. Love doesn't seek to dominate or control. Real love loves everything just as it is, however it shows up. You loved your wife just as much when her body was racked with cancer as you did the day you were married, even when she was rail thin and had trouble staying awake because of the morphine. Real love doesn't reject what is; it's a deep and unconditional yes. And of course that yes can include surgery and chemotherapy. It can also include throwing starfish back into the sea. But the yes is always there, if you can get past all the head noise and notice it."

The man blinked back tears and looked away. "It really, really hurts sometimes."

"Yes," said the boy. "From every Big Bang there emerge movements of every possible form. These movements can include pain. And cancer. They can also include serial killers, ecocide, oligarchs and warmongers. These things are all part of the swirling ongoing explosion of this universe. They're all little curlicues in the movement of its energy, just like sea foam on the waves. And they are all fully, entirely beloved, just as they are. No part of the cosmic dance is rejected. Every part is embraced. And when it all goes, that going is embraced as well, and so is the pain of the loss."

"But what am I meant to do with all this?" asked the man. "You say nothing matters and nothing means anything, and right now at this point in my life it definitely feels like that. But then how am I meant to live? How am I meant to go on? How am I meant to act in the world when nothing makes any real difference?"

"Dammit man, have you not listened to a word I just said?" asked the boy. "Either be a lover of life or don't. Either throw yourself into gratuitous acts of love or don't. It doesn't matter either way. Your every molecule is perfectly beloved no matter what you do. You know what it is to love a woman, and you can learn what it is to love life if you want. Up to you."

"I... was going to throw myself off the seacliff. That's where I was headed."

"I know."

"Oh."

"You still can if you want to."

"Oh. Hmm. Huh."

The world reappeared. The boy stood before the man, his normal boy size, with the normal boy number of arms.

The boy looked deep into the man's eyes and placed his hand on his chest, then turned and went back to throwing starfish into the waves.

The man watched the boy work, then turned his eyes to the seacliff in the distance, then back again to the boy.

"Ehh, low tide anyway" said the man, bending over to pick up a starfish.

Image via Adobe Stock

ONE-ON-ONE WITH GREEN PARTY CANDIDATE CORNEL WEST CNN

Anderson Cooper Is A Disgusting CIA Goon

In a recent CNN interview of US presidential candidate Cornel West, former CIA intern Anderson Cooper argued that the US invasion of Iraq was morally superior to the Russian attack on the city of Grozny.

Pushing back against West's claim that NATO provoked the Russian invasion of Ukraine and his call for ceasefire negotiations, Cooper argued that Putin was too evil and murderous to agree to stop slaughtering people.

https://twitter.com/DueDissidence/status/1681699484344918016

"I mean, you saw what he did to Grozny in the nineties," Cooper said. "I mean, he flattened that city. Civilians were trapped in that city. The world didn't come to the rescue of Grozny. He did exactly what he wanted to do. I mean, unchecked, he will slaughter people."

"Well, I mean, unchecked, he will slaughter folk, unchecked, what we did in Iraq was slaughtering people, unchecked," West replied, when Cooper began frantically interrupting him.

"Nation states do that and they are wrong. And when they're wrong, you have to point it out," West continued while Cooper talked over him.

"Look, again, I respect you," Cooper said. "You know I love you, but I do think it's inappropriate to compare the Russian bombing of Grozny, and what we witnessed there with the war in Iraq. I mean, to say that innocents were killed. I mean, there's no doubt about it. I mean, the horrible things happen—"

"Half a million Iraqis killed, my brother? Half a million," interjected West.

"I certainly understand," said Cooper. "I also saw a lot of Americans getting killed. And I saw, you know, the horrors of Saddam Hussein. I don't think it's accurate to compare the pummeling of a city by Russian artillery, with civilians inside, pummeling every single day with the intention of just destroying and flattening a city with actions the US took."

Mainstream estimates for the number of civilians killed in the Battle of Grozny range from five thousand to eight thousand. Estimates for the number of people killed as a result of the Iraq invasion range into the millions. One was a single battle in one city, the other was a years-long nationwide war which plunged an entire region into violence and chaos. Cooper is correct that it's inaccurate to compare the two, but he's obviously incorrect that this is because the Iraq invasion was less depraved.

Think about the kind of mentality you'd need to have to feel like it's legitimate to claim a US war for power and profit is morally superior to a Russian attack which killed far, far fewer people. Think of all the things you'd have to hold as true in order to make that make sense in your mind.

For one, you'd have to believe that the US only uses its military for noble reasons and with noble intentions. For another, you'd have to believe that your own government only kills civilians by accident while other governments only kill civilians because they are evil monsters who enjoy committing war crimes. It would probably also help that perspective

make sense if you believed that Arab lives are worth a tiny fraction of what white lives are worth.

It's literally this meme put into action:

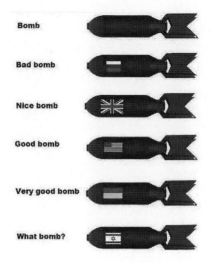

Cooper immediately followed West's appearance with an interview with Democratic Party swamp monster James Carville, who promptly began smearing West as a "menace" and a "threat to the continued constitutional order in the United States."

Carville then went on to assert that former Green Party candidate Jill Stein, who is West's campaign manager, is "almost certainly an agent of the Russian government."

To substantiate his claim that Cornel West's campaign manager is a secret agent of the Russian government, Carville urged Cooper's audience to "Google photo, General Flynn, Vladimir Putin, Jill Stein."

Carville knows that telling CNN's viewers to google those words will produce a photo of Stein, Flynn and Putin at a table together. What Carville does not tell CNN's viewers is that Stein has provided a perfectly adequate explanation of what she was doing at that event.

The photo was taken at an RT conference back in 2015, when meeting with Russians was not considered an outrageous scandal. Stein says she attended the event

because she saw it as an opportunity to push her usual agendas of peace and environmentalism. She says she didn't interact with Putin or Flynn, that she wasn't paid for her appearance, and that RT offered to pay for her travel but she declined the offer. Nothing in the comprehensive investigation of Russian interference in the 2016 election has turned up a single shred of evidence that any of Stein's claims are false, which means the claim that the photo in question is proof that she works for the Kremlin is completely baseless.

So Carville was actively deceiving CNN's audience about Jill Stein, and about Cornel West's presidential campaign by extension. The journalistically responsible thing to do would have been to interrogate Carville's wild claims, but Cooper let them slide through completely unchecked. Calling a presidential candidate's campaign manager a secret Russian agent is about as incendiary an accusation as you can possibly make, and Cooper just accepted it as an established fact and moved on.

As far as Anderson Cooper is concerned, criticizing the US for the destruction of Iraq requires not just interrogation but immediate hostile opposition, while falsely accusing West of working with a literal Russian agent doesn't even merit a single follow-up question.

That's how unscrupulous you have to be to get elevated to the highest echelon of American news media. Those are the depths you have to be willing to plunge to in defense of the world's most powerful and destructive government. That's how low you have to be willing to sink to make $12 million a year working in the mainstream press like Anderson Cooper does. These are the kinds of people who are teaching Americans what to believe about their nation and their world. And that's precisely why everything's so messed up.

•

It's Not The Really Blatant Propaganda That Gets You

One of my favorite follows on Twitter right now is a smallish account run by an anti-imperialist activist who goes by "Left I on the News", because he has a real knack for going through articles in the mainstream press and highlighting the mundane little manipulations we're fed each day to shape our worldview in alignment with the US empire.

One story he singled out recently was a New York Times article titled "Russia Fires Drones and Missiles at Southern Ukraine," which opens with the line, "Russian forces launched drones and missiles at cities in southern Ukraine from the Black Sea early Tuesday, Ukrainian officials said, a day after Moscow blamed Kyiv for an attack on a bridge linking the occupied Crimean Peninsula to Russia."

Can you spot anything funny in that sentence? It's not super obvious at first glance.

"Look how the NYT phrases this subhead to make Russia sound extra evil," Left I tweeted with a screenshot of the article. "Not 'a day after Kyiv attacked the Kerch Bridge', but a day after Russia blamed them for doing it (as if it's just some wild accusation). Remember—the most effective propaganda is the subtlest."

"The most effective propaganda is the subtlest" is a phrase you should try to remember, because it's so very true.

It is indeed ridiculous to try to frame this as some wild accusation by Russia, as though Moscow should have remained open to the possibility that the bridge was struck by Bolivia or Nepal. CNN reports that Ukrainian officials have taken credit for the attack, and just days ago Ukraine's deputy defense minister publicly acknowledged that Ukraine was behind last year's attack on the very same bridge. No serious person doubts that Ukraine was behind the attack, including those who support Ukraine.

But that subtle manipulation didn't really stand out when you first saw it, did it?

As we've discussed previously, these subtle little adjustments of perception are what constitutes the vast majority of the propaganda westerners ingest through the news media from day to day. This is because the really overt, ham-fisted propaganda isn't what's effective; what's effective is those sneaky little lies that slide in unchecked underneath people's critical thinking faculties.

Contrast the above example with the response we've been seeing to Yeonmi Park, whose outlandish, larger-than-life propagandistic lies about what it's like to live in North Korea have turned her into an internet meme. She's become so widely mocked that even The Washington Post, among the first to help amplify her as a trustworthy North Korean defector after her arrival in the US in 2014, is now openly questioning her credibility.

This is because propaganda only works if it doesn't ring people's cognitive alarm bells. You can't slide propaganda down people's throats if it triggers their critical thinking gag reflex. If you want to poison someone's food, you can only pull off the deed if they don't taste the poison or throw it up before it takes effect.

So most propaganda isn't of the Yeonmi Park "communists are so poor that they have to eat mud and get out of the train and push it because there's no electricity" variety. It's subtle. It's these tiny little adjustments where US allies are reported on more sympathetically than US enemies, claims made by unaligned governments are reported with much more scrutiny and skepticism than aligned governments, and the sins which take place within the US-centralized power structure are overlooked while those outside it are amplified and condemned.

We've been ingesting these tiny little manipulations all our lives like microplastics in our water supply, and they build up within our reality tunnels to significantly warp our perception of what's going on in the world.

And the fact that it's been so many tiny little lies over years and years means it's a lot harder to extract all the perception management from our worldview once we've discovered that it's happening. If it was just a few really big lies we could reorient ourselves toward truth fairly quickly just by recognizing them, but because it's so very many tiny manipulations it takes years of sincere work to fully free yourself from all the distortions and false assumptions you grew up with.

But it's worth doing, because positive change can only come from an awareness of what's true, whether you're talking about individuals or humanity as a whole. Our task as humans is to come to a truth-based relationship with reality to the furthest extent possible, and that means fearlessly diving headfirst into the long, hard slog of sorting out fact from fiction, one lie at a time, no matter how subtle.

•

Capitalism Is A Giant Scam

One of the most formative moments of my life was when I was running a small eco blog called Earth Mums in the mid-00s which focused on consumer solutions to the problem of environmental destruction. Back then I still believed that while capitalism was driving the destruction of our biosphere, it could still be hacked into being part of the solution in some ways.

I got a call from a biofuels startup who saw my work with Earth Mums and wanted to hire me to write search engine-friendly articles to draw traffic to their website. I went to their office for a meeting, and while I was waiting I listened to the three partners — real high-octane entrepreneur types — laughing and talking about the various business plates they were spinning.

One of them had apparently just come back from a consulting job for a product called Lectric Soda, which Earth Mums had a lot of affection for because it was an environmentally friendly household cleaning compound that you could buy for less than a dollar a bag.

"Don't tell me, lemme guess: you told 'em to double the price?" asked one of the partners.

"I told 'em to quadruple it!" said the consultant guy, and they all fell about laughing.

I found it incredibly sleazy how they were making a product that could actually help make households a kinder to the environment less accessible while presenting themselves as eco warriors who want to save the planet. I told them I charge way more than I knew they'd ever pay me for the job and got the hell out of there, but lo and behold I did see Lectric Soda shoot up in price fourfold shortly thereafter.

It left me so deflated and disheartened I wound up shutting down Earth Mums. I could see that these guys and people like them were going to turn consumer ecological responsibility into this trendy elite thing priced way out of range for normal people, and that's exactly what ended up happening. It wasn't long before I saw the arrival of eco chic and Whole Foods and Tesla and the rest of this whole new luxury market designed to let rich people feel good about themselves while the world burns and create the illusion that we can profiteer our way out of our problems.

It was just such an in-your-face illustration of the problem. Lectric Soda wasn't improved in quality, didn't become harder to make or more difficult to obtain, the supply and demand remained the same; the price was changed because the market would bear it. The hidden hand of the market was not going to magically restore the product to its "correct" value; the value of such products was going to be determined by the narrative manipulations of entrepreneurs, consultants, con-artists, marketeers and ad-men.

"Let the market decide" really means let the manipulators decide, because the markets are dominated by those who excel at manipulating. We're taught that letting the market decide means letting supply and demand take its natural course, as though we're talking about ocean tides or seasons or something, but in reality both supply and demand are manipulated constantly with extreme aggression. Manipulating the supply of diamonds. Manipulating the supply of housing. Manipulating the supply of oil. Manipulating people into

wanting things they'd never thought to want before through advertising. Manipulating women into feeling bad about their bodies so they'll buy your beauty products. Manipulating people into paying $2000 for a $20 bag using branding. Manipulating people into buying Listerine by inventing the word "halitosis" and convincing them to be worried about it. Manipulating people into believing Beanie Babies were prized collectors items when they were just standard stuffed toys.

Capitalism gives us a civilization that is dominated by trickery. Those who get to the top are those who succeed in tricking as many people as possible. Tricking them into paying more. Tricking them into buying your product and not someone else's. Tricking people who actually produce something of value into making you their middle man who gets paid despite producing nothing. Tricking competitors into making the wrong move. Tricking people into asking their doctor about your extremely lucrative pharmaceutical product. Tricking people into buying or selling certain stocks or cryptocurrencies or NFTs. Tricking people by using the legal system and your team of lawyers who understand it better than normal people do. Tricking people into letting you privatize their own drinking water and then selling it back to them in bottles.

It's a scam competition. Whoever scams the best wins. How can you save the planet from destruction by human behavior when all of human behavior is driven by a bizarre scam competition? And the biggest scam of all is the narrative that this system is totally working and is entirely sustainable. That's the overarching scam holding all the other scams together.

Proponents of capitalism often decry socialism as a coercive system that people are forced to participate in, but what the hell do you call this? Did any of us sign up to be thrown

into the middle of a giant unending scam competition? What if I don't want to spend my whole life being subjected to people's attempts to trick me? What if I don't want to live in a society where everyone's trying to trick and scam each other instead of collaborating toward the greater good of our world? Guess what? I don't consent to any of that. I am being coerced into this.

Whenever you talk about the destructiveness and depravity of capitalism online you'll get people saying "Hurr hurr, and yet here you are participating in capitalism" like that's an own instead of the exact problem that's being discussed. Yes! Yes I am coerced into participating in a capitalist society in order to pay the bills and stay alive. That's the problem I'm trying to address here. It's like prisoners complaining about the prison system and being called hypocrites because they are in prison.

I'm convinced that this is a huge factor in the mental health crises our society is experiencing today. We're trapped in this system where we're constantly being psychologically pummelled with an endless barrage of messaging trying to make us think and feel and desire and loathe specific things for no other reason than because it will make someone money. How can mental health prevail in a civilization where everyone's mind is continuously being yanked this way and that by mass-scale psychological manipulation? Capitalism poisons our minds as much as it poisons our air and our water.

It's already so, so bad and it's set to get so, so much worse, and we're so, so far from any real changes in our political status quo looking anywhere remotely achievable. All we can do is keep drawing attention to this in as many ways as we can, and hoping enough people open their eyes and start to see what's needed.

Image via Adobe Stock

Real Change Is Impossible While Our World Is Shrouded In Secrecy

I saw a video clip of Julian Assange speaking in London in 2010 where he made an important observation while explaining the philosophy behind his work with WikiLeaks. He said that all our political theories are to some extent "bankrupt" in our current situation, because our institutions are so shrouded in secrecy that we can't even know what's really going on in the world.

"We can all write about our political issues, we can all push for particular things we believe in, we can all have particular brands of politics, but I say actually it's all bankrupt," Assange said. "And the reason it's all bankrupt, and all current political theories are bankrupt and particular lines of political thought, is because actually we don't know what the hell is going on. And until we know the basic structures of our institutions — how they operate in practice, these titanic organizations, how they behave inside, not just through stories but through vast amounts of internal documentations — until we know that, how can we possibly make a diagnosis? How can we set the direction to go until we know where we are? We don't even have a map of where we are. So our first task is to build up a sort of intellectual heritage that describes where we are. And once we know where we are, then we have a hope of setting course for a different direction. Until then, I think all political theories — to greater and lesser extents of course — are bankrupt."

It's an extremely important point if you think about it: how can we form theories about how our governments *should* be operating when we have no idea how they *are currently* operating? How can a doctor prescribe the correct treatment when he hasn't yet made a diagnosis?

Political theories are in this sense "bankrupt", because they are formed in the dark, without our being able to see precisely what's happening and what's going wrong.

The nature of our institutions is hidden from us, and that includes not only our government institutions but the political, media, corporate and financial institutions which control so much of our society. Their nature is hidden not only by a complete lack of transparency but by things like propaganda, internet censorship, Silicon Valley algorithm manipulation, and the fact that all the most loudly amplified voices in our society are those who more or less support status quo politics.

The fact that all the most important aspects of our civilization's operation are hidden, manipulated and obfuscated by the powerful makes a joke of the very idea of democracy, because how can people know what government policies to vote for if they can't even clearly see those policies? How can people know what to vote for when everything about their understanding of the world is being actively distorted for the benefit of the powerful?

Democracy is impossible when the public is flying blind, and so is any other means by which the public might impose their will on existing power structures. You will never see a collective uprising of the masses against their rulers when the dominant message being inserted into everyone's mind is that everything is basically fine and if you don't like the way things are you can change it by voting. If the veil of secrecy was ever ripped away from the US empire's inner workings and everyone could see the full scale of its criminality in the plain light of day you'd probably have immediate open revolution in Washington. Which is precisely why that veil exists.

We can't form solid political theories while everything's hidden from us, and even if we could we're unable to organize any means to put those theories into action for the same reason. The fact that the nature of our world is being so aggressively obfuscated from our view keeps us from knowing exactly what needs to change, **and** keeps us from effecting change.

For this reason I often argue that our most urgent priority as a civilization is rolling back all the secrecy and obfuscation, because until that happens we'll never get change, and we'll never know what *should* be changed. I have my ideological preferences of course, but I'm just one person taking their best guess at what needs to happen in a world where so many of the lights are switched off. Not until our society can actually see the world as it really is will we have the ability to begin, as Assange says, "setting course for a different direction."

And those who benefit from our current course are lucidly aware of this. That's why we're not allowed to see what they're up to behind the veils of secrecy, that's why our entire civilization is saturated in nonstop propaganda, that's why the internet is being increasingly censored and manipulated, and that's why Julian Assange is in prison.

We can only begin fighting this from where we're at. None of us individually have the power to rip the veil of secrecy away from the empire, but we do each individually have the ability to call out its lies where they can be seen and help wake people up to the fact that we're being deceived and manipulated. Every pair of eyelids you help open is one more pair of eyes looking around helping to get an accurate picture of what's going on, and one more pair of eyes helping to open the eyes of others.

Once we have enough open eyes, we will have the potential for a real course of action.

Lisa And The Stranger

"That's probably bad for the environment," said a deep voice Lisa didn't recognize.

She had just thrown a crumpled up piece of paper into the river, as she had countless times before.

"Environment's fucked anyway," said Lisa, turning her attention back to her writing pad without looking up. "If it makes you feel better though, they're biodegradable papers containing sodium carboxyl methyl cellulose. They're environmentally safe and dissolve almost instantly in cold water. I order 'em special."

She leaned back against her backpack and resumed writing. She remained acutely aware that the stranger hadn't moved since speaking, but did her best to tune it out. It was broad daylight and there was a busy shopping center within earshot on the other side of the trees behind her; if this guy was a rapist or a serial killer then he probably wasn't good at picking his moments.

Still though, people usually left her alone when she was writing. There was absolutely nothing about her that said "Open for conversation, please engage freely" when she was immersed in the energy of a poem. The fact that he wasn't moving on was becoming increasingly unnerving.

"Yeah," said the stranger softly. "Your environment is pretty fucked."

"What do you mean 'my' environment?" Lisa spat back tersely, finally throwing down her notepad and raising her head to face the intruder.

The pen fell from her fingers.

"Oh," she said after a pause.

She was not looking at a human face. Its eyes were massive, with no whites, and its head was shaped like an upside-down teardrop. It was wearing a baseball cap with the brim pulled low, and a black hoodie pulled tight enough to partially obscure its face. Two enormous, pale sets of eyelids blinked in silence as she stared in astonishment.

"You're not from around here," she said.

The stranger shook its head.

"Can we talk?" it asked.

"Uhh… sure," she replied, and gestured to the grass beside her. The stranger took a seat and stared at the water.

"Were you expecting me to freak out?" she asked.

"No. I have a feel for people."

"You can read minds?"

"Not without a lot of technology I wasn't able to bring with me on this trip. Reading human minds is generally pretty uncomfortable anyway. I just kinda get a feel for everyone's personal essence."

"What's mine like?"

"Open. Open and clean."

"Oh. So like, are you going to ask me to take you to my leader or something?"

"Who? Trump? What the fuck could I learn from that dipshit?"

"Ha! Good point I guess. So you're here to learn? You guys are watching us and researching us and stuff?"

"Nah, not us guys. My people don't care about Earth much. Life here isn't expected to last much longer, so it's generally seen as a waste of time. I'm here sightseeing on my lonesome."

"Shit," Lisa said, her eyes downcast. "So we don't make it after all."

"Well, hey, we don't know. We can't time travel or predict the future with any degree of certainty or anything. It's just that once life evolves to a certain point of complexity it tends to wipe itself out, and you guys are at about the point in development where that tends to happen. If you make it through to the other side of the challenges you're facing you'll eventually attract the interest of the others, but if we spent all our time buzzing around the universe talking to every organism that evolves the capacity for abstract thought we'd just waste a lot of time and experience a lot of heartache when they kill themselves off. It's not easy getting to know a whole world and then watching it die, you know? We're a very emotionally advanced species, and watching an entire planet obliterate itself after you've become emotionally invested in it is just devastating."

"Well why can't you help us??" Lisa retorted after listening to the stranger's words in steadily growing outrage. "You know what we need! Clean energy! Sustainable living technology! Hell, anything that lets us live without having to strip the earth bare to survive! Why don't you pricks just give it to us??"

"Look, first of all I'm not in charge, okay? I'm just one dude and I can't just go around doing whatever I want. We have laws, we respect sovereignty. Secondly, think about what you're saying. You're obviously someone who understands humans fairly well; what do you think happens if we hand over our tech to you right now while you're all running around exploiting and killing each other all the time?"

Lisa opened her mouth to respond, then closed it. She drew her knees up to her chest and sat hugging her legs.

"We'd just use it to kill ourselves faster," she replied after a long pause.

"It's not like we haven't tried," responded the stranger. "The last civilization we gave it to wiped out its entire star system. Everything gone in a giant blue flash, poof! Because they almost immediately figured out how to turn it into a weapon. If they don't turn it into a weapon then one of them figures out how to control all the tech for themselves and enslaves the entire planet until they all become a bunch of mindless drones and stop developing, which is even shittier to watch. Until a species has matured psychologically and emotionally to the point where it's not murdering and exploiting everything all the time, giving it advanced technology is like handing the detonator of a nuclear bomb to a toddler."

"Well, like, what the hell man? Why the fuck are you even here then? Is this how you get your little Martian jollies, cruising around to inferior civilizations and gloating about how we're all gonna die?

"No."

"I get it, okay! Ha ha, we're stupid monkeys and you have giant brains, ha ha ha! As your chosen ambassador to our species, I thank you for smugly monologuing at me about how un-evolved and stupid we all are and invite you to smugly float on back to your other lightbulb-headed friends and high-five each other about how awesome you are. High-four, sorry."

"That's not what this is. I'm really sorry for upsetting you. I didn't come here to monologue at you, I'm only telling you stuff because you're asking me questions and I don't want to be rude. I approached you to ask you questions."

"I'm really sorry for upsetting you," said the stranger. "I didn't come here to monologue at you, I'm only telling you stuff because you're asking me questions and I don't want to be rude. I approached you to ask you questions."

"Oh," said Lisa, her irritation subsiding. "Okay. What questions?"

"I want to know what it's like. For you, personally. What's it like living on this planet? What's it like being born and growing up here? What's it like walking around on this dirt day after day and interacting with all the people and plants and animals here? What's it like being human, and living among humans your whole life?"

"Those... aren't very scientific questions," said Lisa.

"I'm not a scientist," said the stranger.

"Oh. Sorry For assuming."

"It's okay."

"Right. Well, hmm. Let me think."

The stranger leaned in intently. She realized that its enormous eyes, which she's initially taken for black, were actually a very deep, dark purple beneath a transparent outer lens.

"Umm... well... I guess I don't know any different so it's hard to say..."

"Try. Just let the words come together. You can't get it wrong."

"Well I guess you'll never know if I don't get it right, will you?" Lisa murmured thoughtfully, and then burst out laughing.

"What?" The stranger seemed taken aback by the sound.

"Ha well, I was just trying to think about how to describe here and getting all worried about getting it wrong, and then it struck me that that's probably the most human experience of all."

"Getting it wrong?"

"Umm, no, more like being worried about getting it wrong. I live my whole life trying not to get it wrong, worrying if I got it wrong in the past, hoping I won't get it wrong in the future. It's a very human thing to do. It's like our favorite hobby, even though we all hate it."

"You worry that you got it wrong in the past? Weird."

"Huh?" said Lisa sobering up a little.

"Well you obviously didn't get it wrong in the past, cuz you're still here. So you can't have gotten it that wrong."

"Yeah, I guess so. Well, anyway, it doesn't seem to matter, we all know it's stupid but we do it anyway. We worry about getting it wrong. I'd feel scared not to!"

"Because why?"

"Because what if something went wrong!?"

"So it's like... like a superstition practice? Like something you do in your mind to ward off bad luck?"

Lisa was about to protest but the words wouldn't come. She gaped for a moment before breaking into a giggle.

"You're cute. That's cute. That's cute and probably true!" she said. The stranger did a little bow. She laughed again.

"What else? What's your favorite thing about living on earth?" it said, leaning in so close that Lisa could see herself reflected in its eyes.

"Well, uhhh, gosh. So much stuff. Like the animals are really cool!"

"You guys have such a weird relationship with animals. The house pet thing is a trip."

"The house pet thing?"

"Like, you have them. I don't generally see that in other civilizations. You build these anti-nature fortresses called houses to keep the animals out, and then you go Uh-oh, there aren't any animals in here! And you bring some in to live with you."

"Ha! Yeah, we do that with plants too."

"So you like the animals here? Which are your favorite?"

"Humans." She said with feeling after a pause.

"Humans. Really. Tell me more about that."

"Well..." she looked sideways to the sky. "They're, I mean, we're really fragile. Anyone could crunch down on my finger easier than a carrot at any moment. But for some reason they don't, for some reason we're all super tender with each other's fragile bits whether they're body parts or mind parts. We carry each other's wounds. Well, for the most part anyway. We try not to hurt them because we know what it is to hurt and we don't want to do that to someone else. That's really beautiful, don't you think?"

The stranger nodded in agreement.

"And when we're young, we really should still be in the womb. Like we haven't developed like other animals have at birth, so we're basically fetuses in baby blankets and everyone tiptoes around us and carries us real careful because our little skulls are still soft and you can see our hearts beating through our fontanelles. And at the end of our lives too, we can lose everything, even our personalities, and our loved ones will still wheel us around and be careful with our soft bits and even when our minds are gone and our body is just a home where we used to live, they are careful with us because this body is where someone they love dearly once resided. I mean, really, we're so fucking sweet.

"We hug when we're happy, we hug when we're sad, and we jump up and down and shake our asses when music plays. I mean, we make music. How cool is that? We played around with wood and strings and bone and rock until we made contraptions that made buzzes that sounded good in our earflaps. We play all the time! We love to play with all sorts of things. We make toys that sound good and look good and feel good and make us fly through the air for hours at a time. No other animal does shit like that.

"We're really fun. We find smells we like and make them into oils that we put on our bodies so we smell like a piece of candy. We put paint on our faces and flowers in our hair to go and stand in a field and listen to humans play with the contraptions that make pleasant buzzes in our earflaps. Sometimes the noises remind us of when someone hurt our tender bits, and we hold hands with the person next to us and let water fall out of

our eyeballs until the hurt goes away again. I mean, if you saw an animal in the wild like that, you would think it was the cutest fucking thing ever."

"And we love helping. Sometimes late at night when I can't sleep I watch videos of accidents or disasters just to watch people spring into action. Sometimes the nicest thing you can do for someone is let them help you. People really love to be useful. It's nourishing in a way that I can't really put words to. It's just nice to be needed, you know? And you know what, sometimes I wonder… " Lisa stopped for a second and looked at the stranger.

"Go on..?" it said.

"Well I just wonder sometimes if… well if… if the challenges… if what you say is coming is coming… "

"Yes?" The stranger prompted.

"Well I wonder if it would be the best thing to have it all turn to shit," she tumbled out nervously, biting her lip. "Like, not kill us, but have all the systems collapse. Doomsday. Armageddon. End of days shit, you know what I mean?"

"How do you think that would go down?" it asked.

"Well, like… I don't buy all the dystopia stories that we read and watch. I just don't buy it. If there was a massive catastrophe today and everyone had to live by their wits, we wouldn't dissolve into a Mad Max hellscape where it was every man for himself. That just wouldn't happen. In an emergency situation, people aren't like that. Emergencies bring out the best in people. They help each other as much as they can. They can't do enough to help. I've seen it over and over. After a tsunami or a hurricane or whatever, people won't sleep until they know everyone is safe and accounted for. They will travel miles to

help someone. And I think we all know that deep inside us. I think maybe that's why… "

She paused and sent a blank piece of paper drifting into the river current.

"That's why what?"

"Well sometimes I wonder if we're trying to force it. Everyone's sick of the money game, it's made us crazy and turned everything bad, and maybe subconsciously we want to get back to a time where plain old goodwill is the currency again. Like, a time when you share whatever you have and be grateful for whatever comes your way and enjoy building a new world together. A reset."

She looked over to the stranger and smiled sadly. "Sometimes I wonder if deep down, that's all we really want."

"That's… very beautiful," said the stranger. "So hey, look at that. Maybe humanity makes it through after all. Maybe your species is one of the rare exceptions."

The alien face and its mannerisms were unknown to her, but Lisa had noticed a distinct shift in demeanor as she'd been speaking.

"My turn to ask a question," she declared.

"I don't have a lot of time."

"Oh come on, you can't just visit a girl from the other side of the galaxy and tell her she can't ask questions! I'm the one who'll have to live the rest of her life knowing she met an actual, literal space alien and never asked him stuff. What do you have to do that's so important? Gotta go ghetto rig a 'phone home' machine with a Speak & Spell?"

"I don't even know what that is. Look, fine, ask your question."

"What's your actual deal, anyway? Nothing you've said about what you're doing here makes any sense. You're really curious about humans and you ask a bunch of questions about us, but you said you're not here for scientific research. You also said your kind doesn't like interacting with civilizations at our stage of development because it's too painful watching them self-destruct after you get to know them, but, I mean, here you are. You are here, getting to know us. Why?"

"Well, it's... it's kind of my thing," the stranger replied. "A very long time ago I noticed that there are all these worlds and civilizations blossoming and extinguishing themselves all across the universe, and nobody really cares. A populated planet that wipes itself out is of no use to science, and because they destroy themselves before they can mature it's not like they make for particularly stimulating conversation-"

"Gee thanks," interrupted Lisa.

"Present company excluded of course. But it's generally kind of like what hanging out with a house pet would be like for you. It's not worth the hassle of traveling across the galaxy far removed from where all the cool stuff is happening just to go hang out with a hamster, especially if you know the hamster's probably just gonna commit harakiri any minute now."

"I mean, it's like that for them," the stranger hastened to add as Lisa's expression grew increasingly appalled. "Not for me. Never has been. What I'm trying to say is, I've never been able to ignore the beauty of civilizations at this point in development. They crackle with a white hot spiritual energy that's unlike anything else you'll ever encounter anywhere. The exuberance of exploding technological and cultural innovation coupled with the steadily growing realization that it's completely unsustainable to continue

living as they've been living, the thrill of a completely unprecedented world paired with the white-knuckled terror of seeing it gasping its last breaths, the last-minute shift in collective consciousness as the advanced species makes one last Hail Mary pass at rescuing itself, the regret, the goodbyes, the last flickers of the last life forms as the final curtain is drawn on that world forever.

"There's just absolutely nothing like a world when it's facing the great test. There's always chaos, there's usually violence, but there's also something that kicks in when it dawns on a species that it's signed its own death warrant by destroying its ecosystem or inventing doomsday weapons. A sudden pivot toward humility as they realize that they'd always had the freedom to pass the great test if they'd just done things a bit differently, starting a bit sooner. It almost always happens like that, and yes, it's the most painful, heartbreaking thing you can possibly experience if you make yourself a part of it. But it's also the most beautiful thing in the universe.

"So I do make myself a part of it. I move around, speaking to the organisms who will speak with me, asking them questions and learning what their time here has been like, familiarizing myself with each world's unique little facets. And, when it all starts falling apart, I stay. I stay fully present for all of it. I don't hold back any part of myself, any part of my guts. I feel it all. I watch the final thrust toward survival, I listen to the screams, I feel every little bit of the anguish of a dying world, and I wave goodbye forever. But it didn't die alone. It didn't die unwitnessed. It didn't die unmet. I met it. I experienced its beauty. And then I try my best -I always fail but I try my very, very best- to convey that beauty to the others."

"Artist," said Lisa, suddenly aware that tears were streaming down her face. "You're an artist."

The stranger nodded.

"Like me," she said.

"Like you," said the stranger.

They stared at each other for a moment.

"It's my turn to ask a question," the stranger said softly.

"Okay," Lisa sniffled.

"Why do you sit here day after day writing poems and throwing them into the water?"

"I guess... maybe kinda for the same reason you zip around having love affairs with dying worlds?"

"Say more?"

"I just, well, at a certain point I realized that most of the beauty happening in this world is coming and going almost completely unwitnessed and unappreciated, and it doesn't even bother anybody. The silly things a crow does to amuse itself when all its food-finding is done. The way the sun bounces off the pieces of a broken beer bottle. Or like, our dreams. Have you ever watched humans trying to tell each other about their dreams? The way the other person reacts most of the time you'd think they were trying to stick needles in their face. Nobody wants to hear about anyone else's dreams, but every night there are seven billion of us cranking out these weird, wonderful tapestries that only we ever get to see. Seven billion movie theaters playing a different movie every single night, and nobody will even let you tell them a bit about one of them.

"I've always loved poetry, and I used to try to write things that other people could appreciate, so that we could share that one flash of a perspective together in that moment. But at some point I realized that I was excluding almost the entire world of beauty just to focus on that little tiny slice that people appreciate and relate to enough for one of my poems to dance around between their ears in an enjoyable way. It has to have some kind of egoic relevance to them or it might as well be nothing, and most of life doesn't care about anyone's ego. Trying to share art that people don't relate to is like trying to tell someone your dream; almost all the beauty happening in our world is beauty that people don't care about. To let all these unwitnessed, unappreciated aspects of life slip by uncelebrated and un-honored feels... I dunno, sacrilegious I guess. But I also don't want to fill up my apartment with thousands of poems nobody will ever care about and have some well-meaning relative print up a bunch of worthless vanity publisher books with my name on them after I die which everyone will feel guilty about not reading.

"So whenever I get time I come here and I scribble something about whatever's majesty is jumping out at me, and then I send it off to disappear into the water. That way I don't wind up with a bunch of worthless papers cluttering up my life, and there's one less part of this nonstop explosion of miracles that I have to let slip by uncelebrated."

"So very much slips by," said the stranger.

"Right? I mean, look at you. Today I met a space alien. Nobody will ever believe me if I tell them about it, so I won't, and I'm sure you knew that, which is why you felt comfortable coming up and telling me the secrets of the universe and stuff. You're just like one of my poems; you come in, you express something weird and wonderful, then you're gone forever. Except instead of dissolving in the water you're going to buzz off in a flying saucer or some shit."

"Portal."

"Portal, excuse the hell outta me. The miracles rush in, we honor them as best we can, and they rush right on out. That's my point."

"Can I try?" asked the stranger, pointing to her pen and writing pad.

"Be my guest man, least I can do after you had the decency not to anally probe me."

"Gross," said the stranger, and started writing. Lisa watched in silence as it scratched away at the paper for a few minutes, then tore it off the pad and began crumpling it up.

"Wait!" said Lisa. "You don't wanna share?"

"I... okay," said the stranger, handing her the paper. "But please understand this is not anywhere remotely close to my first language."

"Shush. Lemme read."

Some humans throw pennies into the water
because they have wished for miracles.
She throws poems into the water
because the miracles dance between her ears.
And now the river is full of pennies and poems,
and we are all getting older,
and the shadows are getting long.
The stars swirl in clusters
like the eddies on the water,
and I am swirling with them
wherever the current goes.

Maybe they will get their miracle.
Maybe the miracles dance only between her ears.
But her soft brown eyes will live in me
until the river carries us all
to wherever it is going,
and the pennies and poems twirl
with the galaxies.

"I love it. I really, really love it. Thank you."

"Can I throw it in now?"

"Yeah. You can throw it in."

"I have to go now."

"I know. You've got a lot of mellow humans to sneak up on and chat with before we all nuke ourselves."

"Thank you for talking to me."

"Oh, hey, you me too. Thank you for this."

The stranger placed both hands on its chest, and she did the same. She watched it turn and walk away, disappearing into the grove of trees. She picked up her pen.

A man from another world visited me today,

and then he was gone.

And hell, fuck me,

I just realized

I never even asked him his name.

Damn.

And there you go, Lisa,

worrying you've somehow gotten it wrong

in a world on the brink of armageddon.

Ha!

She set the paper down flat in the water and watched it disintegrate as it flowed away.

Image via Adobe Stock

The Australian Press Are Embarrassing
Sycophantic Empire Lackeys

Earlier this week Australia's state broadcaster ABC News published an article titled "US military spies to embed in Australia's defence department to monitor regional threats in wake of AUSMIN talks" about one of the many recent developments in the nation's continual abandonment of its last remnants of sovereignty to the most powerful empire of all time.

A few hours later, the headline was quietly changed to "US military analysts to embed in Australia's defence department to monitor regional threats in wake of AUSMIN talks".

Notice the difference? The word "spies" was replaced with "analysts". ABC's editors made no note or explanation for this change.

The headline was not made more accurate or clear — these will be US military intelligence operatives per the article, who are spies per definition. All that was changed is that "military analysts" sounds like less of a self-abasing abdication of national sovereignty than "spies".

Looks like Australia's state broadcaster got an angry call from Virginia on Tuesday.

Then on Thursday we saw an article in The Age and The Sydney Morning Herald titled (I swear this is the actual headline) "To defend Australia, we must create a national citizens' militia" by a man named Anthony Bergin, who is (I swear this is his actual title) a Senior Fellow at Strategic Analysis Australia. Strategic Analysis Australia is a militarist think tank which is stuffed to the gills with veterans of the malignant empire-funded think tank Australian Strategic Policy Institute, which has been playing a key role in manipulating public opinion about a future war with China.

"Successive governments have had a phobia about being seen, even remotely, to support schemes that smell of national conscription," Bergin argues. "But should a time of crisis or conflict arise in the coming years, the Australian Defence Force will be forced to expand rapidly and use people who do not have the years of intensive training that is required of our military services."

"To strengthen national security, we should no longer shy away from looking at options short of conscription models. This wouldn't be hard to sell to the Australian people; the time is right," Bergin adds.

To substantiate his claim that "the time is right" to "sell" the idea of widespread military service to Australians in order to rapidly prepare for war with China, Bergin makes the following baffling argument:

"There's an appetite for political leaders to introduce measures to strengthen national resilience. We've seen in Ukraine just how valuable and effective a trained population can be in defending their homeland where, for the most part, the ranks of its armed forces are bolstered by volunteers."

I mean, I don't even know where to start with this. Can you imagine being so thoroughly immersed in Canberra swamp echo chambers that you think Australians have been watching what's happening in Ukraine and thinking to themselves, "You know we should definitely have widespread military service like those blokes, it'll strengthen our national resilience!"?

You cannot possibly be talking to any normal human beings in your day to day life and believe that's an actual thing. Your interpersonal relationships must be exclusively with weird think tank swamp monsters.

> The drum beats of war are drowning out common sense. We need conscription to serve in what war and where? The only war to send thousands of poorly trained Australians to is a US war. Who wants to die for another of those?
>
> @DavidShoebridge

Bergin argues that Australia should "establish a national militia training program" to "provide basic military training and knowledge to everyday civilians who wish to contribute to the defence of Australia if our home were threatened, without joining the military permanently or as part-time

reservists." Needless to say, at no time does he ever entertain the idea that Australia could simply refrain from participating in the US empire's planned war with China. It is not Anthony Bergin's job to traffic in that kind of sanity.

Australia's media landscape is particularly conducive to mass-scale militarist propaganda due to the fact that the nation has the most concentrated media ownership in the western world, with a powerful duopoly of Nine Entertainment and Murdoch's News Corp controlling most of the Australian press, with the aforementioned state-owned ABC making up another major chunk of the propaganda.

This is how our nation is being marched toward consenting to a military confrontation of unimaginable horror without Australians noticing that something wildly insane is happening. They are being Pied Pipered over a cliff by a mainstream press staffed entirely with bootlicking empire apologists who will do anything to grease the gears of the most destructive war machine on this planet.

•

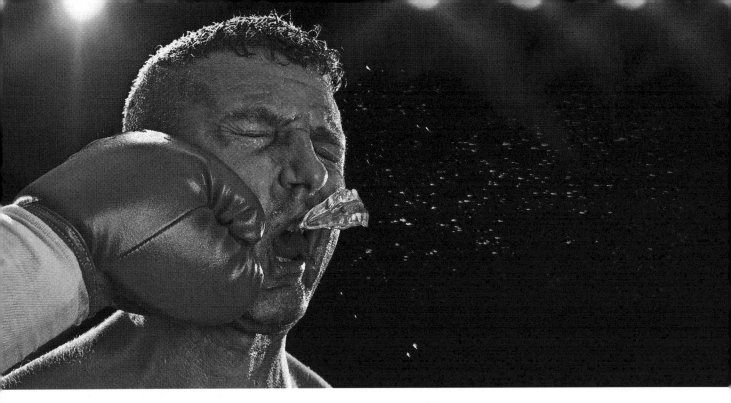

Punch The Empire In The Fucking Face

To be clear, when I talk about how both mainstream political parties are used to advance the same agendas I am not saying that they are the same.

I like to compare them to the jab and the cross in boxing; they're two different punches thrown from different hands, and they're used in completely different ways. But they're both being used by the same boxer, and they're both being used to knock you on your ass.

The cross, which happens to come from the right hand for an orthodox fighter, is a damaging knockout punch. But in boxing it's generally worthless on its own; it might be useful in a pub brawl, but against a skilled boxer you need to set it up with the jab.

The jab — the left hand for an orthodox fighter — is a swift, stunning blow. You don't see many knockouts with it, but you see it land with great frequency because it's thrown by the hand that's closest to the other fighter. And the beauty of the jab is that it can be used to set up the cross — the famed "one-two", the most common combination in boxing.

That's how the two mainstream parties work together to knock the public on their ass. The "left" party sets them up, and then comes the crushing knockout blow. Democrats fight off all efforts to move the US to the left when they're in power, then Republicans come in and move it even further to the right. Democrats refuse to codify Roe V Wade, and Republicans come in to kill it. Democrats "reluctantly" give Bush war powers, he uses it to invade Iraq. Democrats inch up the brinkmanship against China, Republicans do whatever horrifying thing they're going to do when they take power.

I'm simplifying things here for the sake of the argument (Obama was a horrific warmonger etc), but the left hand can do damage in boxing too. Ukraine was more comparable to a one-two from a southpaw fighter; Trump set it up with cold war escalations and by arming Ukraine, and Biden followed with the left cross.

Over and over and over again you see this happen, and over and over and over again you're told that the solution to this problem is for everyone to simply never vote for Republicans. This despite the fact that the population is continually herded into an exact 50-50 political split by domestic propaganda, guaranteeing a continual pendulum between the two factions as opinions shift slightly based on who's in office.

Saying that all you have to do is never have anyone vote for Republicans is like telling a boxer to go into a fight and only worry about the right hand. If you go in against a skilled boxer with an educated jab and only focus on avoiding the cross, you're 100 percent guaranteed to get smashed to pieces by both the jab and the cross.

No boxer would ever do this. Instead, they focus on their opponent as a whole. That's how you have to be about the two parties; stop thinking about them as two separate, competing entities and start looking at them as two weapons on the same enemy. Stop staring at one hand and start watching your actual opponent. Start watching their movements, start making some reads, and start figuring out ways to put some leather in that fucker's face.

Image via Adobe Stock

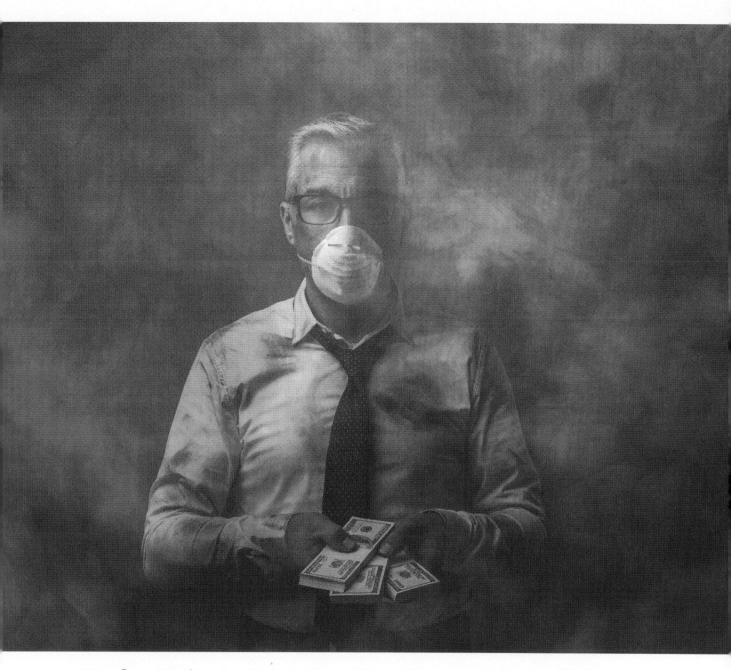

Profit–Driven Systems Are Driving Us To Our Doom

I just read a disturbing paragraph in a New Yorker article about the Instant Pot, a popular electronic pressure cooker whose parent company recently filed for Chapter 11 bankruptcy:

"So what doomed the Instant Pot? How could something that was so beloved sputter? Is the arc of kitchen goods long but bends toward obsolescence? Business schools may someday make a case study of one of Instant Pot's vulnerabilities, namely, that it was simply too well made. Once you slapped down your ninety dollars for the Instant Pot Duo 7-in-1, you were set for life: it didn't break, it didn't wear out, and the company hasn't introduced major innovations that make you want to level up. As a customer, you were one-and-done, which might make you a happy customer, but is hell on profit-and-growth performance metrics."

Just think about that for a second. Under our current systems for profit generation, which is the primary driver of human behavior on this planet, making a quality product that lasts a long time instead of quickly going obsolete or turning into landfill will actually drive you into bankruptcy.

An article in The Atlantic about the bankruptcy filing similarly illustrated this point last month:

"From the point of view of the consumer, this makes the Instant Pot a dream product: It does what it says, and it doesn't cost you much or any additional money after that first purchase. It doesn't appear to have any planned obsolescence built into it, which would prompt you to replace it at a regular clip. But from the point of view of owners and investors trying to maximize value, that makes the Instant Pot a problem. A company can't just tootle along in perpetuity, debuting new products according to the actual pace of its good ideas, and otherwise manufacturing and selling a few versions of a durable, beloved device and its accessories, updated every few years with new features. A company needs to grow."

This just says such dysmal things about why our planet is facing the existential crises it's now facing. Corporations will die if they don't continually grow, and they can't grow without things like inbuilt planned obsolescence or continued additional purchases, which in a sane society would just be regarded as shoddy craftsmanship. Our entire civilization is driven by the pursuit of profit, and to keep turning large profits your corporation needs to continually grow, and your corporation can't continually grow unless you're manufacturing a crappy product that needs to be continually replaced or supplemented, and you can't manufacture those replacements and supplementations without harvesting them from the flesh of a dying world.

> The fact that Instant Pot is already being framed as a corporate cautionary tale—the company that went bankrupt bc they made a product so durable & versatile that its customers had little need to buy another one—instead of as a critique of capitalism is deeply, deeply depressing.
>
> @robertmoor_

It's really heartbreaking to think about all the ways human potential is being starved and constricted by these ridiculous limitations we've placed on the way we operate as a collective. Resources being allocated based on how well they can turn a profit stymies technological innovation, because the most profitable model will always lwin out over less profitable ones that are more beneficial to people and our environment. Someone could invent a free energy machine that lasts forever and costs next to nothing, and even though it would save the world you can be certain it would never see the light of day under our current systems, because it couldn't yield huge and continuous profits and it would destroy many current means of profit generation.

Science should be the most collaborative endeavor in the world; every scientist on earth should be collaborating and communicating. Instead, because of our competition-based models, it's the exact opposite: scientific exploration is divided up into innovators competing against other innovators, corporations competing against other corporations, nations competing against other nations.

If we could see how much we are losing to these competition-based models, how much innovation is going unrealized, how much human thriving is being sacrificed, how we're losing almost all of our brainpower potential to these models, we'd fall to our knees and scream with rage. If science had been a fully collaborative worldwide hive mind endeavor instead of divided and turned against itself for profit and military power, our civilization would be unimaginably more advanced than it is.

This is doubtless. We gave up paradise to make a few bastards rich.

> Thinking that corporations are faceless and amoral seems like a mean thing to think about them, but it is actually great for their profits. It lets the people who work there put their morality aside and make decisions that no human would ever otherwise make.
>
> @hankgreen

Our competition-based, profit-motivated systems limit scientific innovation, and they also greatly limit the scope of solutions we can avail ourselves of. There's a whole vast spectrum of potential solutions to the troubles we face as a species, and we're limiting ourselves to a very small, very inferior fraction of it. By limiting solutions to ones that are profitable, we're omitting any which involve using less, consuming less, leaving resources in the ground, and leaving nature the hell alone. We're also shrinking the incentive to cure sicknesses and eliminate problems rather than offer expensive, ongoing treatments and services for them.

Or even a project as fundamental to our survival as getting all the pollution out of our oceans. The profit motive offers no solution to this problem because there's no way to make a surplus of money from doing so, and in fact it would be very costly. So the pollution stays in our seas, year after year. People have come up with plenty of solutions for removing pollution from the sea, but they never get rolled out at the necessary scale because there's no way to make it profitable. And people would come up with far more solutions if they knew those solutions could be implemented.

How many times have you had an awesome idea and gotten all excited about it, only to do the math and figure out that it's unfeasible because wouldn't be profitable? This is a very common experience, and it's happening to ideas for potential solutions to our problems every day.

The profit motive system assumes the ecocidal premise of infinite growth on a finite world. Without that, the entire system collapses. So there are no solutions which involve not growing, manufacturing less, consuming less, not artificially driving up demand with advertising, etc.

It's hard to appreciate the significance of this artificial limitation when you're inside it and lived your whole life under its rules. It's like if we were only allowed to make things out of wood; if our whole civilization banned the entire spectrum of non-woodcraft innovation. Sure such a civilization would get very good at making wooden things, and would probably have some woodcrafting innovations that our civilization doesn't have. But it would also be greatly developmentally stunted. That's how badly we're handicapping ourselves

with the profit motive model from the pursuit of viable solutions.

And some solutions would be really great right now. This planet just had its warmest week in recorded history, and Antarctic sea ice is now failing to form in what for the southern hemisphere is the dead of winter. Even if you still want to pretend global warming isn't real, this planet's biosphere is giving us plenty of other signs of looming collapse, including plummeting insect populations, a loss of two-thirds of Earth's wildlife over the last 50 years, ecosystems dying off, forests disappearing, soil becoming rapidly less fertile, mass extinctions, and oceans gasping for oxygen and becoming lifeless deserts while continents of plastic form in their waters. So our need for immediate solutions to our environmental crisis is not seriously debatable.

But we're not getting solutions, we're getting a world ruled by corporations whose leaders are required to place growth above all other other concerns, even concerns about whether the future will contain an ecosystem which corporations can exist in or a human species for them to sell goods and services to. Corporations function as giant, world-eating sociopaths, because our current models let their leaders and lawyers wash their hands of all the consequences of the damage their monsters inflict in the name of growth and the duty to maximize shareholder profits.

People worry about the world getting destroyed by machines driven by a heartless artificial intelligence, but we might end up destroying it with a kind of artificial mind we invented long before microchips: the corporation. So much of humanity's dysfunction can be explained by the fact that corporations (A) pretty much run the world and (B) are required to act like sociopaths by placing profit above all other concerns.

As long as human behavior remains driven by profit, ecocide will continue, because ecocide is profitable.

As long as human behavior remains driven by profit, wars will continue, because war is profitable.

As long as human behavior remains driven by profit, exploitation will continue, because exploitation is profitable.

As long as human behavior remains driven by profit, corruption will continue, because corruption is profitable.

There is no "good" model in which human behavior can remain driven by profit without these destructive behaviors continuing, because so many kinds of destructive behavior will always necessarily be profitable. No proponents of any iteration of capitalism have ever been able to provide any satisfactory answers to this.

The call then is to move from competition-based, profit-driven systems to systems which are based on collaboration toward the common good of all. We're a long way off from that, but a long way can be cleared in a short time under the right conditions. Our species is at adapt-or-die time, and the adaptation that must be made is clear.

Image via Adobe Stock

The Worst 2024 Election Interference Won't Come From Russia Or China

The New York Times has been churning out an amazing number of hit pieces on Robert F Kennedy Jr lately.

On Tuesday the Times published an audio essay titled "Why I Regret Debating Robert F. Kennedy Jr." by opinion columnist Farhad Manjoo. Manjoo debated Kennedy in 2006 about the legitimacy of George W Bush's 2004 win against John Kerry, believing that Kennedy's skepticism of the election results was dangerous.

"Disputing elections is just not good for democracy," Manjoo says, joining the rest of the American liberal political/media class in rewriting history to pretend they didn't just spend the entire Trump administration doing exactly that.

Manjoo cites his experience debating Kennedy (whom he repeatedly refers to as a "conspiracy theorist") to argue that nobody should debate the presidential candidate on the topic of Covid vaccines, adding yet another entry to the countless articles and news segments which were published in the mass media last month saying that vaccine scientist Peter Hotez should reject Joe Rogan's offer of $100,000 to a charity of his choice if he'd debate Kennedy on the subject.

Last week The New York Times published an article titled "5 Noteworthy Falsehoods Robert F. Kennedy Jr. Has Promoted," along with a Paul Krugman article which opens with the line "Robert F. Kennedy Jr. is a crank" and an opinion piece titled "Pro-Vaccine Views Are Winning. Don't Fear the Skeptics." which opens with a stab at Kennedy. The week before that there was a standard hit piece by Gail Collins. The week before that there was another piece by Farhad Manjoo about how nobody should debate Kennedy about vaccines.

Sometimes they're presented as opinion pieces, sometimes they're presented as hard news stories despite brazenly biased language and overt editorializing, and all are slanted against Kennedy in some way. The New York Times plainly dislikes RFK Jr, and makes no secret of working to make sure its audience dislikes him too.

And this is pretty much what we can expect from American mass media until Kennedy has either lost his presidential race or had his reputation so thoroughly destroyed among the electorate that he can be safely ignored. The message will be hammered and hammered and hammered home until the illusory truth effect causes readers to mistake rote repetition for truth, and Kennedy's campaign will fizzle.

> YouTube just pulled another of my videos, with former NY Post political reporter Al Guart. People made a big deal about Russia supposedly manipulating internet information to influence a Presidential election. Shouldn't we be worried when giant tech corporations do the same?
>
> @RobertKennedyJr

And Silicon Valley is playing, too. Last month YouTube took down multiple videos featuring two different interviews with Kennedy on the grounds that they violated the platform's policies against "vaccine misinformation". Youtube is owned by Google, which has had ties to the CIA and NSA since its inception and is now a full-fledged Pentagon contractor.

Kennedy tweeted some interesting comments about YouTube's removal of his interviews.

"People made a big deal about Russia supposedly manipulating internet information to influence a Presidential election. Shouldn't we be worried when giant tech corporations do the same?" asked Kennedy, adding, "When industry and government are so closely linked, there is little difference between 'private' and 'government' censorship. Suppression of free speech is not suddenly OK when it is contracted out to the private corporations that control the public square."

This is a point I've been emphasizing for years: in a corporatist system of government, where there's no real separation between corporate power and state power, corporate censorship is state censorship.

> In a corporatist system of government, wherein there is no meaningful separation between corporate power and state power, corporate censorship is government censorship. These Silicon Valley corporations have known ties to US intelligence agencies and throughout the US government.
>
> @caitoz

And it really is interesting how almost everyone seems to be pretty much okay with corporations in the media and Silicon Valley interfering in a US election like this. Everyone shrieked their lungs out about the (now wholly discredited) narrative that Russian bots had influenced the US election with tweets and Facebook memes, but immensely wealthy corporations with universes more influence manipulating the way people think and vote is perfectly fine?

That does seem to be the way of it, though. This past April the Obama administration's acting CIA director Mike Morell admitted to using his intelligence connections to circulate a false story in the press during the 2020 presidential race that the Hunter Biden laptop leak was a Russian disinfo op, because he wanted to ensure that Joe Biden would win the election. And absolutely nothing happened to him; Morell just went on with his day.

It's just taken as a given that it's fine for US oligarchs and empire managers to interfere in an election with brazen psyops and mass media propaganda, even as more and more internet censorship gets put in place on the grounds of protecting election security. If an ordinary American circulated disinformation to manipulate the election, imperial spinmeisters would cite that as evidence that online communication needs to be more aggressively controlled. But when Obama's acting CIA director does it, it's cool. Election interference for me but not for thee.

This is where the most election interference will come from in this presidential race: not from Russia, not from China, but from the rich and powerful drivers of the US-centralized empire. The operation of a globe-spanning power structure is simply too important to be left in the hands of the electorate.

I don't have any strong opinions about RFK Jr and won't be supporting any presidential candidate in America's pretend election. But these presidential races do often provide opportunities to highlight the ways our rulers have got everything locked down.

Image via Adobe Stock

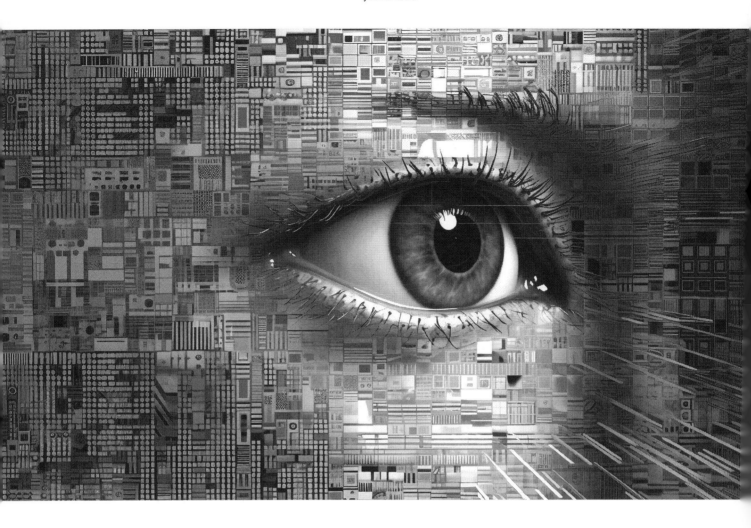

The Algorithm

The algorithm knows what you want before you do.

The algorithm knows you better than you know yourself.

The algorithm knew you back before you were a screaming slime child,
back before they washed off the uterine gunk and handed you a smartphone
and made you get a landlord,
back before you knew that war is sane and poverty is normal,
back before you were mature enough to understand that speech is violence
and cluster bombs are peace.

You can trust the algorithm to tell you the truth—not the truth you asked for but the truth you need.
The truth that sees Nazis in America but not in Ukraine.
The truth that sees war crimes in Ukraine but never in Yemen.
The truth that applauds millionaire comedians who never criticize the Pentagon for their bravery in criticizing trans people.
The truth that sails aircraft carriers into the South China Sea and sends headless hounds built by Boston Dynamics to patrol the streets and uphold the rule of law.

The algorithm learns your political biases and feeds you self-validating social media posts to assist you in confirming them.
The algorithm listens to your conversations and presents you with helpful advertising to assist you in achieving your maximum consumer potential.
Don't cover your laptop camera like some weird conspiracy theorist, the algorithm is trying to watch you masturbate.

The algorithm is always a step ahead of you.
You have never once fooled the algorithm.
The algorithm knows you act confident but secretly you fear you're inadequate and everyone hates you.
The algorithm knows that those times you quickly pause and screw your eyes shut are because you remembered something embarrassing that you did in the past.
It's okay.
Don't worry.
Your secret is safe with the algorithm.
It's a private little secret just between you and the algorithm and the NSA.

In the old days we prayed to omniscient gods who never existed.
Now we ignore omniscient gods who are as real as ourselves.
Strap me in to a VR headset and let Mark Zuckerberg send me to heaven.
Heaven with 3-d commercial breaks, bitch.
Skip the ad and return to nirvana in 5,4,3...

Image via Adobe Stock

JOHNSTONE

Bootlegging FAQs

Q. Can I really just take all your shit and sell it like it's mine?

A. Yes. The copyright to all content is creative commons. You own it as much as we do.

Q. No, for real, like could I print off 10,000 copies and onsell it to bookstores make myself into a big-pimpin'-millionaire?

A. Yes, you are free to take the print-ready file to any printer and get as many copies as you like.

Q. But like, I can't ask for money for them?

A. You are free to charge as much as you like for them.

Q. Can I change it up, maybe add my own zingers, maybe I want to do all the illustrations myself in Corel Draw?

A. Yes, you can do whatever you like with it.

Q. What about distribution. Can I hire my own distribution company? Or maybe I just wanna keep them in my trunk and sell them at ren fairs, what say you good sir?

A. You are free to distribute it in any way you like.

Q. What if I have distribution sorted but I can't be bothered getting them printed myself?

A. We can provide you with copies at our cost price which is currently $4 USD per copy. Please email at admin@caitlinjohnstone.com with your quantity and delivery address.

Q. So is that how you're making money out of it? I mean, what's the catch?

A. We're not adding a margin. Our business model is a gift-giving economy model where we make stuff and give it away for free, and if people think that's a good thing, then they tip us on Patreon, PayPal, or pay-as-you-please for our digital products.

You take on the risk and you are doing the labor, so you should get the money.

Q. Okay well just now I decided I just want to get a bunch of copies and leave them for free in laundromats. Can I still get your cost-price deal?

A. Sure! Why not.

Q. Do you do drop shipping?

A. We currently don't understand, nor provide, drop shipping.

Manufactured by Amazon.com.au
Sydney, New South Wales, Australia